To Paula,

Someone who has been there all through the discovery period! May your talents continue to shine.

\# friend \# coach \#teacher
\# HR \# patience \#kind

Love,
Michael

PRAISE FOR *TAGGING FOR TALENT*

This unique way of integrating talent identification into the learning arena is not only innovative, but fun. Employees are able to recognize each other for what they do well and not just what their manager thinks they are good at. This opens up a completely new world of opportunity for both the individual as well as the organization and give Human Resource professionals more talent to work with.

> **- Rhonda Bernard**
> Director of Learning and Talent Management,
> Estee Lauder Companies Europe

Tagging for Talent help brings the identification and classification of talent and potential into the 21st century, by giving HR professionals and Managers a modern tool to track and unearth an organization's untapped talent. In today's biased war for talent, having blind cvs and tools from the last century aren't enough. This tagging approach will help women and minorities get discovered, promoted and developed by harnessing the power of the crowd and removing layers of bias.

> **- Anne Ravanona**
> Founder & CEO, Global Invest Her

These ideas demonstrate a practical way to put employees first. By giving co-workers the opportunity to identify internal talent, they provide a reliable source of intelligence for the company. Ultimately, the customer wins.

> **- Vineet Nayar**
> Author of *Employees First, Customers Second*

Tagging for Talent offers hope for how HR professionals and business leaders can create better competence networks that will improve talent processes. Michael's decades of experience help him envision the potential of this innovative technological approach to improving talent management. Such insights are central to HR's creating new solutions to talent challenges.

- Dave Ulrich
Rensis Likert Professor, Ross School of Business,
University of Michigan, Partner, The RBL Group

Tagging for Talent puts forth a groundbreaking approach for companies and organizations to utilize peer-to-peer collaboration in its rawest form. Key words that give both value and recognition when used in this context help all parties succeed on a variety of levels. A must read!

- Soumitra Dutta
Dean of the SC Johnson College of Business at Cornell University
and co-author of *Throwing Sheep in the Boardroom:
How Online Social Networking Will Transform Your Life, Work and World*

Michael stands out as a model exception amongst HR professionals because he adeptly connects the dots between HR and business. He fully understands that whatever HR does has to be relevant to the business and add value. This book is the latest great example of Michael's passionate commitment to value creation. It is a must read for any company looking for an innovative approach to Talent Management.

- Edward A. Trolley
Senior Vice President, Consulting & Advisory Services at NIIT
and co-author of *Running Training Like a Business:
Delivering Unmistakable Value*

Tagging for Talent is fascinating, engaging, and incredibly practical. Michael Salone shows us a way forward in identifying and leveraging talent across an organization, challenging many of the assumptions we have about talent systems and processes, from identification to succession and everything in between. It's a must-read for HR practitioners and people leaders alike.

- Mike Pino
Senior Digital Learning & Technology Strategist, GE

Michael Salone was able to infuse meaning into the abstract concept of tagging. I believe that his book highlights a real solution, not just a new trend related to a soon-to-be-obsolete technology. *Tagging for Talent* is highly ground-breaking and definitely the way that many managers should think about their approach to promoting or hiring people in their organization.

- Hugues Foltz
VP Professional Services, Optel Group. Former President, CEO, Ellicom

Tagging for Talent:

The Hidden Power of Social Recognition in the Workplace

Michael Salone

Made for Success
PUBLISHING

Library of Congress Cataloging-in-Publication data

Salone, Michael

    Tagging for Talent: The Hidden Power of Social Recognition in the Workplace/ Michael Salone
    p. cm.
    ISBN-13: 978-1-61339-898-2 (HRDBK.)
    LCCN: 2017905985

To contact the publisher, please email service@MadeforSuccess.net or call +1 425 657 0300.

Made for Success Publishing is an imprint of Made for Success, Inc.

Printed in the United States of America

10 9 8 7 6 5 4 3 2 1

DEDICATION

To the many HR people who work hard and play a difficult role...
To my good and bad managers who shared by example...
To my mentors and coaches and family and friends,
this book is a result of your influence...

To the crowd...

WARNING! BEFORE YOU READ THIS BOOK

HR professionals, sit down and take a deep breath.

CEOs and managers, be prepared to listen carefully.

Employees, you're now in charge,

because what you are about to read

can change the way you view and identify talent forever.

Contents

INTRODUCTION

I t's no secret that subjects like how to become a millionaire, lose 20 pounds or attract a mate make perennial bestselling books. Another book about talent management? Snore. You'd probably rather tackle Tolstoy's *War and Peace*. Well, the boring HR book cliché ends here because what I am about to present takes this topic to a whole new level. It dares to bring humanity back into the workplace by catalyzing the power of individuals to be recognized and recognize others for their whole potential. I believe the concept you will learn about has the potential to shift the talent paradigm. When I discovered it, I couldn't believe that it wasn't already being put to use. The whole reason why I ventured into writing this book was to share the idea; it's a concept that works well, delivers real-time results and is fun and easy to use. Sometimes, the best solutions are the simplest.

Let's face it – no matter how much we try to democratize talent management and succession planning, it's "the boss" who is in control (and by "boss" I mean anyone who has the authority to dish out raises, organize your work schedule or wield power over your next promotion). But what if everyone played a role in creating a new workplace reality? In this reality, everyone's potential is visible, and future leaders can be found in perhaps the most unlikely corners of the organization. This new workplace includes a practice that, over time, will lead us to identify our future bosses and leaders, individual contributors, and those who are the best organizers, administrators, linguists, engineers and such within a company. It taps into the organization's collective knowledge of individuals so that we can all identify the competencies and strengths of those around us – whether we're based at the company headquarters or in a remote location, selling our ideas to the board of directors or Skyping from home. What I'm prescribing here is a benevolent, above-board approach to identifying and retaining talent – with some of the end results being happier employees, more flexible work teams, cheaper systems, simpler processes and greater profitability. The underlying goal of this approach is to make the talent pools in organizations more visible more quickly and, in the process, help to foster personal growth and career fulfillment.

To be clear, I am not a university professor with five sets of credentials after my name; I'm also not a twenty-something computer whiz or MIT savant with a Cupertino corner office. I'm a career-long HR professional who has observed and participated in the entirety of the HR spectrum. I've hired, fired, graded, noted, promoted, inducted, red-circled, quoted, changed, engaged, surveyed, appraised, reviewed, quality circled, Six Sigma'ed, nine-boxed, visioned, missioned, mobilized, oriented, expatted and re-patted, outsourced, outplaced, right-sized, downsized, gain shared, profit shared, job shared, welcomed and exited along with the best of them. (And yes, thousands of fully buzzword-compliant books have been written about these things.) In the talent management arena, I've covered the gamut of mentoring, coaching, training and development; I've facilitated, succession planned, career pathed, talent reviewed, people reviewed and Corporate U'ed. I jumped out of bed every morning like a dedicated HR soldier, intent on finding a better way to do all of the above in its current context, but it became clear to me that today's employees and boards expect much more.

As difficult as it is for many of us in the Human Resources profession to admit, we have re-scoped, re-analyzed, re-engineered and even gone as far as to re-title ourselves in an effort to "build a better HR mousetrap." What has become obvious over time, as we've attempted these reinventions, is that we're constantly trying to fix things that don't work as well as we'd like them to. A lot of well-meaning HR professionals, line managers, and service providers have developed a series of solutions that aim to change the way we identify and manage people drastically, but oftentimes do no more than put a temporary patch on the problem. We have tried to solve problems such as whether to tell our key employees if they are high potential or not, inform our people of their roles in succession plans and assess who is eligible for that great new leadership program we just launched. These questions have been debated for decades at conferences, meetings and in our daily business activities. Nowadays, the forum for these debates has evolved into online discussion groups, with millions of people and consultants weighing in with their opinions of the same old mousetrap.

There's another way, a *much* better way, to identify the talent that companies already have but can never seem to find quickly enough, assess accurately enough, develop adequately, motivate and retain. To take the next step is primarily a question of courage. CEOs are already prepared to take the leap, as they have long been dissatisfied with the length of time it takes to identify resources for key roles and projects, the constant demand to launch another leadership program and the costs associated with heavy support systems.

During the interview for my very first job out of college, like every other gung-ho, naïve HR candidate, I told the interviewer that I wanted to work in this profession because "I'm good with people." (In spite of that answer, I got the job.) In the eons that have passed since then, my most gratifying days are still when I am able to match someone's talent to a job, recognize that person for his or her skills and see the person advance in his career or reach her fullest potential. If I could have that kind of impact on even more individuals, with a direct impact on operational performance, I would be closer to the dreams I had when I first began my career. What if being "good with people" was the right answer to that interview question after all, not the inside joke that it is today?

TAGS THAT TALK

CHAPTER 1

I couldn't believe what I was hearing. After years of developing the latest and greatest HR information system and working daily to get people to use it, we *still* were not getting the data we needed. This realization became obvious yet again one day while in a monthly meeting with the top HR professionals of a *Fortune 500* company with more than 100,000 employees. The discussion had just turned to some excellent news for the business – and the staffing headache this latest milestone was causing.

"I'm thrilled to report that we have recently won several top money contracts in Brazil," announced the Chief HR Officer. "Unfortunately, getting qualified labor to staff the projects will be very difficult. We've got quite a large staff in Brazil already, but finding people to take on some of these jobs will be very difficult."

Now, I was aware that this organization had spent more than $20 million dollars on its sophisticated HR information system (HRIS) and that what was spent didn't include an equal amount or more spent on "running costs," deployment, communications, and upgrades over the years. I also knew they had a structured succession planning and talent identification process in place. So it seemed strange to me that they wouldn't have already had some qualified individuals inside the company to staff these contracts.

I wondered if the CEO was aware of this lack of return on his investment. So I asked an obvious question: "Have you looked *inside* to see if any of your current employees might have emigrated from Brazil?"

The response was somewhat obtuse: "Of course we did. We only found three people inside the company who speak Portuguese."

"How did you determine that?" I asked.

"Well, we looked at our people database, and that's what came out."

"Is it possible that some of those who left Brazil might have adopted new nationalities or even changed their names?" I continued.

And the response: "Well if they don't enter it in the *system*, how are we supposed to know?"

What struck me is how so much effort is spent by corporations to identify talent, measure performance, incentivize, train and put in place all kinds of programs — and yet they still cannot find the people they're looking for. It's a system that is highly inefficient when you think about it.

The above scenario is something that I have encountered time and time again. Companies rely on their internal "specialists" or sophisticated processes to know the people they employ, while other employees assimilate this knowledge every day. So it occurred to me: If we could come up with a way to allow employees and their peers to share their knowledge of each other through their daily experiences, while also capitalizing on the increasing use of online collaborative tools, we might just get this whole talent identification thing right, once and for all. This book is a result of that rumination.

Integral to the approach I am presenting here is a Web 2.0 feature called "tags," a concept that has been around for decades and is proliferating in the world of social media (more about all of this in a minute). These little ditties seem harmless enough and quite benign; but tags, as I see them, can wield great power. Could they also unlock the key to the cavernous vault of company database information and render it more useful? What if a process existed whereby employees could tag their colleagues (and thus their future leaders) with descriptors of their talents and competencies? At a minimum, it would represent an entirely new use of social media that satisfies both the skeptics of its business applicability and the adopters who use it daily. It could also help to define a whole new generation (and future generations) of HR experts, create a way for employees to recognize each other's strengths and provide a motivating element to the workplace.

This book explores tagging within an organization and its potential for very positive effects on costs, time, quality and employee recognition – something sorely lacking in today's business models. Most importantly, it puts internal competency identification into the hands of those who are probably best qualified to make the observations. Consider this: the colleague who you tag today could be your (or someone else's) boss tomorrow. By the same token, the tags that you receive today could become the impetus that encourages you to go in a different direction than the standard "career path" you've been on; those same tags could become the catalyst that propels you to the top of your organization because now you've been noticed.

In the coming chapters, I will discuss how to tap the collective intelligence of individuals with the use of tagging to identify better, match, recognize and retain talent, as well as significantly reduce HR time and costs. The results can be transformational, partly because tagging catches employees doing something right on a real-time basis (by their peers) instead of evaluating their deficiencies in one annual performance review (by their bosses). No doubt, the tagging approach will cause concern for traditional HR folks and great promise for those whose charge is to be innovative. And employees? They'll be asking: "What took so long?"

Tags: Labels With Leverage

You may or may not already know what tags are. For such a tiny thing, it's a huge topic with many particularities. To ensure that we have a common understanding, let's look at tags and how they're typically used. By tagging, I am not referring to the game where children (or some inebriated adults) chase each other until someone is caught, at which point the pursuer yells: "Tag! You're it!" I also don't mean graffiti artists who "tag" city walls, bridges, and buildings with spray paint. I also don't mean tags as clothing labels or price tags. I am talking specifically about tagging as it is used in software applications and social media: keywords or terms that are used to label, identify and search online for information, friends, photos, files, bookmarks and other content. This "metadata," or "data about data," helps to describe an item and allows it to be found again by somebody else simply by browsing or searching for the word or label given. Tags are so simple to create that anyone can do it; there is really no learning curve involved.

If you're familiar with blogs then it's quite likely that you've already come across what's known as a "tag cloud," or a graphic made up of all the keywords or labels that have been identified in the authors' posts. The size of each word indicates how many times the label or keyword was given, so viewing the tag cloud gives an immediate "picture" of the blog's content and each label's apparent importance.

PinterestLinkedIn InstagramSnapchat Baidu Twitter Classmates Etsy QZone Yelp OkCupid WeChat Sina Skype Line Facebook Meetup Tumblr Tinder WhatsApp Viber

You may associate tags with labeling the location of a photo and the people in it. But this labeling can go beyond name and location. You and others can label a photo with the food that was eaten, the weather of that day, historical tidbits you've learned about the place, a color that is prominent in the photo, or whatever other associations it brings to mind. You may have already come across this type of tagging in some popular photo software applications such as Picasa, iPhoto, Flickr, FOAP, Instagram, and others. People like the simplicity of tagging because it's practical. Compare having to put photos into a traditional paper photo album versus keeping a digital library of your photos.

Tagging can be used to label, identify and search online for basically any kind of information or content, not just photos. Twitter users tweet using hashtags to label groups and topics. It has been enormously successful with bloggers and researchers, as well as anyone selling or purchasing products or services online. Bloggers, as noted above, can create "subject" tags for topics covered on a blog or Web page. Wikipedia authors can tag information throughout their documents so that others can find and add to the content. In Zazzle, people upload products they've created and tag them with single words like "holidays," "calendar" and "beach," so they show up in the Zazzle marketplace (as well as search engine searches) and buyers can find them. With Flickr, users can not only harness tags to sort and manage their own photos but also use tags to find similar photos from other users. In Trip Advisor, one can tag that "great resort in Bali" that didn't quite live up to the travel agent's description by rating the food, service, ambiance, and price using multiple words or phrases. Some tags are purely administrative in nature and only meaningful to the individual who creates them – for instance, the name of a project to which a resource was relevant, a "task list" or "unread" notice to remind the user to take some sort of action.

So many people are into tagging that a somewhat formalized methodology—a "folksonomy," as coined by information architect Thomas Vander Wal—has been created by folks getting together online and determining a classification system for managing tags. Whereas the origin of tags was meant to help people find information across a variety of platforms, the folksonomy phenomenon is, in itself, quite fascinating and now speaks to the power of individuals – or, more accurately, the power of the crowd. As we'll explore next, it's also about to rock the HR world.

> /folksonomy/ derived from the Greek *taxis* (classification) and *nomos* (law), and the Old English *folk*, or people. The term *folksonomy* (a combination of *folks* and *taxonomy*) was first credited to Thomas Vander Wal. *Taxonomy* is the practice and science of classification; and a folksonomy is a Web-based, user-generated classification that emerges through the use of labels (or, tags) created by those who are actually using the resources that it classifies, such as online photos, web links, and other content.

Shaking Up the Status Quo

> "Indeed, self-organizing communities on the Web have proved time and time again that they can be more effective in creating value than hierarchies – so why should it be different in the workplace? As self-organization becomes accepted as a viable method of production, more and more workplace processes will move from being hierarchically directed to self-organizing."
>
> **—Don Tapscott and Anthony D. Williams**
> *Wikinomics: How Mass Collaboration Changes Everything*

Granted, tagging your photos is fun or being tagged in a blog can be useful, but these applications of tagging aren't necessarily going to transform your career. Tagging your skills and competencies at work? Now there's something that has the potential to change a great deal about your life. So, let's get into how tags can be used to identify and recognize talent and explore why a new approach is even worth considering.

As you've probably deduced by now, one of the amazing things about tagging is that it enables a massive amount of information to be found readily by anybody who is looking for it. While this is completely obvious today as we search for information online, it seems to have been overlooked in people identification practices. Think about it: In 10 seconds or less we can track down statistics about something as complicated and far away as the Sombrero Galaxy, which is 28 million light years from Earth; however, it can take weeks, months, even years to find the right talent match inside a company—and sometimes we're not successful in doing so at all. We go through umpteen administrative rigors to identify replacements for key jobs, anticipate successors for crucial positions and determine which employees have the highest potential within an organization. Simply put, if we can find what we're looking for from our home computers in a matter of seconds, it seems feasible that we should be able to find it from our desks.

Humor me a bit with the following crazy analogy that really isn't so different from what happens in large companies. Imagine that you're a CEO in a helicopter, hovering over the stadium during the Super Bowl or Rugby World Cup—or, if you prefer, a rock concert. You can see your star players in the center of the field, or lead singer on stage, fully visible even from 10,000 feet. But you also have 50,000 fans in the stadium. Some are weekend warriors who play in amateur football clubs and weekend pick-up games—or, garage band junkies who get the neighbors riled up as they play loud music late into the night. All have some kind of potential, whether it's to be a player on the field, a musician on stage, or to play a critical role in supporting those out front. But it's physically impossible to see all of these people from your so-called vantage point in the air. So, being the smart CEO that you are, you employ agents, recruiters, and scouts to seek talent and identify potential replacements for that star player, for example, who might succumb to an injury or be lured away by a better contract.

Now imagine you're that same CEO in a company of 50,000, 25,000 or even as few as 50 employees. How could you possibly know all of those people? You know your "top players" and "rock stars," of course, dedicating time and resources to develop their skills and abilities. Most likely, you've also employed talent scouts or talent managers (as they tend to be called in a company) to seek out potential replacements for your top team members, specialists or experts. Now let's throw in another factor: The people in your organization are most likely not sitting all in one place like at a concert hall or football stadium; they're probably spread out in different locations around the city, country or world. With that, the challenge of "knowing your people" becomes even more complicated. This analogy may seem to be a stretch, but you get my point. Large organizations have limited "real" visibility of their entire "stadium" of people (including the talent they *do* know) even with the processes they have in place to make it easier to find them. Therein lies the problem, and the reason why a better solution is needed.

To further make my point about why we need to shake up the status quo, here's an example about one of the processes that are currently in place for many companies. You may know it as the proverbial spreadsheet exercise. I facetiously call it the "Succession Leadership and Organization Worksheet"... or, SLOW... or, SLOP, if you use PowerPoint. It's SLOW because it takes so long not only to complete them but to actually access and use the data they hold to identify talent succession within an organization adequately; SLOP because we then hurriedly try to put it all together for a presentation that the bosses will understand. While some companies have moved onto utilizing faster and exorbitant HRIS systems, many are still SLOW-ed down by the exercise itself. How often do you actually turn to that SLOW document when something unplanned happens with someone on your team – an illness, resignation or role change, for instance? Do you ever think: *Hold on! I've got data on that sheet we did 12 months ago. Let me look and see who the replacement is.* If your company is like most, you have found that the SLOW exercise probably doesn't justify the time and effort put into it. Sure, it may be well-organized SLOP with beautiful photos and impressive detail —all meant to get managers thinking about their succession plans—but it's sometimes brokered by an HR department that is forced to formalize a process that goes on without them. I do believe the spreadsheet exercise is implemented partly as a way to encourage managers to talk about their people. In many organizations, this isn't done enough, so the value of the process may not actually be in succession planning, but rather in teaching managers that the phrase "our people are our most important asset" is more than just a noble slogan.

A Blue Ocean of Talent

One of the benefits of my working in the learning and development area of a large company was the exposure I had meeting, working with and becoming friends with some of the world's smartest minds in business, leadership, and human behavior. I'm thinking now of a time in 2005 when I had taken a team of potential senior executives from my company to a program being held at the Singapore campus of the international business school INSEAD. My friend and colleague Dr. Narayan Pant, then the dean of executive development, was presenting one of many dynamic, interactive sessions over the course of the three-week intensive program.

It was shortly after the launch of the groundbreaking book *Blue Ocean Strategy* by W. Chan Kim and Renée Mauborgne, and Narayan was teaching a strategy session based on this book. Kim and Mauborgne got businesses thinking differently about how to compete in new spaces. Their book's subtitle says it all: *How to Create Uncontested Market Space and Make the Competition Irrelevant.* Who wouldn't want to know how to do that? They demonstrated why companies could no longer expect long-lasting, profitable growth simply by battling in the same "red ocean." Only by developing new "blue ocean" marketplaces could they expect to succeed over the long term.

As I sat in the back of the room at Narayan's lecture, I listened as he attempted to get my company's future leaders to consider how our large industrial B2B could think like a Starbucks or Cirque du Soleil. I heard participants say things like: "That might work with cappuccinos and clowns, but our customers are different." I scratched my head, wondering how these young potential senior executives within our company could already be tainted with the "we've always done it this way" syndrome so early in their careers. Unfortunately, I'd seen this same scenario in the HR profession many times before, especially when it came to talent identification. It seemed simple enough: To more effectively find people, we needed to think differently and compete in new spaces. I envisioned this new space as the "Tagosphere," and I will invite you into it during the upcoming chapters.

As I listened to Narayan's lecture on *Blue Ocean*, I thought about all the reasons why these same concepts could – and *should* – be applied to talent identification. Let's face it: big companies seem to spend a lot of time battling their own internal issues of politics, territory, and ideas when the real competitor is just outside waiting to swoop in. I don't care if you're the market leader in your industry, your employees are prime for the picking no matter how successful you are – no, scratch that – *especially* when you're successful. We often think of the customer as being outside of the organization, but when it comes to talent, we have "buyers" every day wanting the services and know-how of our teams. Not having informed knowledge of the talent pool at your fingertips becomes not just detrimental, but in some cases, fatal to the company.

Sailing Along with Current Processes

Before we can don our Ray-Bans and speed full throttle into the Tagosphere, it's important first to take a closer look at some of the current processes being used. Only then will any of what I'm about to suggest, make sense for putting in place a plan of action. Let's begin by defining the term "talent management."

What is talent management? Is it the handling of Hollywood A-listers? No, although it can feel that way at times when dealing with the egos of some of our star performers. I'm referring to the whole gamut of "hire-to-fire" processes, or just being uniquely responsible for a specific population of employees. Talent management can be restricted to a specific department in a company's HR strategy or promoted as "it's every manager's job to manage talent." For this book, think of talent management as a combination of activities that are supported by a variety of processes that aim to identify, attract, retain, develop and promote individuals within a company. I'll break this to you gently: rarely do these activities originate solely from a company's altruistic intentions. The aim is usually to support the organization's business objectives as a whole.

The talent management process sounds congenial, but I have seen it become quite ferocious. The need to attract and retain employees—whether the economy is slumping or skyrocketing—can be highly competitive, hence the phrase "war for talent." The profession has seen new job titles popping up every day: Chief Talent Officer: VP of Workplace Excellence: Talent Management Manager; VP of Talent Management; Head of People Acquisition; Director of Organization Capability; and the list goes on.

Regardless of the job title, let's cover a few key steps in the talent management area so that we have a common view. Whether you're working in HR and striving to make these processes work, or a member of management trying to follow the rules, most companies today have one or more of the following processes, and it may look something like this:

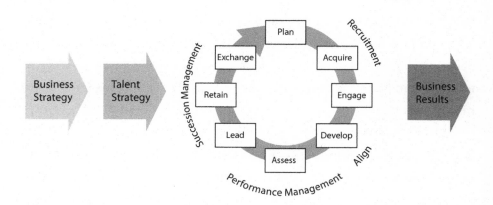

Obviously, a lot of sub-processes exist under each of these. For simplicity's sake, I will focus on only a couple for now, as we'll touch on the rest a little later when we discuss the benefits of tagging.

Recruitment: This process is usually placed at the beginning or end of the Performance Management cycle. A recruitment is made (either internally or externally) based on a need to fill missing skills within the organization. Whether through the creation of a new position, the lack of a suitable successor, or an uptick in business, the recruitment comes down to a missing or anticipated need for certain skills.

Performance Management: For simplicity, I'm going to group Objective Setting, Periodic Reviews, and Performance Evaluations together under the umbrella of Performance Management. Employees are generally handed down a set of objectives or targets from the top of the organization, based on a combination of goals or aims that it wishes to achieve. The method for establishing these objectives varies from company to company, with some allowing for bottom-up participation, group objectives or other variances on the theme. These objectives are usually some combination of behavioral and job-specific (that is, functional or technical) and can be adjusted over the year during the periodic or mid-year review. While we're on the subject, the HR ritual that every employee and manager unceremoniously abhor is the Performance Evaluation. (No? Come on! Admit it.) Even if many employees appreciate the opportunity to receive feedback and see how they're doing, this face-to-face meeting is, hands down, the most uncomfortable process in the HR cycle for all concerned. Okay, salary negotiations can rank right up there, but when it comes to that meeting with the boss at the end of the year to *evaluate* our performance, even when it's been outstanding, we just want to get it over with. And if managers of strong teams feel uncomfortable watching nervous employees squirm or defend their results for the year, then imagine what it's like for managers of difficult people.

The Performance Management cycle is intertwined with the evaluation of competencies, learning and development needs, mobility wishes and other very important discussions—which, of course, vary among companies.

Some companies provide opportunities for feedback from more than the boss through a 360° Review process or tool, but oftentimes this is limited to a small percentage of the employee population and is highly monitored and controlled. In the end, while the recipient usually appreciates the results, the once-a-year feedback is too infrequent to make an impact. This annual event (even as we work to train managers to have these discussions every day) is basically a "wrap up" of the year and preparation for the next.

Succession Planning / Talent Review: This is the culmination of the entire Performance Management cycle, where managers assess their teams' performance, competencies, risks for attrition, mobility needs and desires while designing replacement plans. Think of succession planning as the method by which companies identify their "bench strength" and determine what needs to be done to develop their people. It increases the visibility of experienced and capable employees who are prepared to assume new roles as they become available, or outlines the steps necessary to prepare employees for career moves. Succession Planning can also help identify missing resources, and it usually governs the identification of replacements —specifically, what kind of replacement, when the person might be available, and whether the person is cross-functional or has leadership potential. This review takes place in a variety of ways, generally with a process title that is something like "Talent Review" (see SLOP, above).

Career Path / Plan: It may shock you when I say that career planning, as it's done currently, is outdated for today's (and certainly tomorrow's) workforce, but please hear me out. While Career Paths or Plans are good at giving individuals a possible direction, especially for certain job functions or industries (think technical career ladders), the best days for these kinds of structures have come and gone.

As a manager, it may be my good intention to lay out a long-term plan for my employees to aim for, but any sudden change in structure, shifting market dynamics, technological evolution, customer demands or any other number of variables can make this plan not only outdated but unpredictable, at best. Add to this the fact that we want employees to be flexible and ready to change at a moment's notice (or when the company changes directions), and it's no surprise that employees expect the same of management. These days, it is not unusual for employees to think of their career plans in one-year increments. Gone is the emphasis on interview questions such as: "What do you want to do in 10 years?" Young graduates are taught in school how to answer this question but chances are these new entrants to the workforce will get bored far quicker than that and won't be patiently waiting beyond a year or so for the right opportunity to present itself. Even if an organization sets its sights on the long-term, more and more employees are thinking short-term.

Organizations that still believe in the "she-should-stay-in-her-position-for-at-least-three-years-to-be-sure-she-learns-the-job" mindset are sadly out of touch with employee expectations. When an employee of such a company *does* decide to leave, the company is (surprisingly!) surprised. "We gave her such a great opportunity!" they say. "If only she'd been more patient." The truth is that if we don't help employees evolve more quickly than *we* expect and focus on what *they* expect, they will take matters into their own hands, which may mean moving on to another position or organization. The old adage, "Putting the right person in the right place at the right time" (also known as, "We'll take the right person to go to the middle of nowhere as soon as we can find them") might need to be reprioritized. Instead, we should be asking: "Have we got the right place for the right person in the shortest amount of time?"

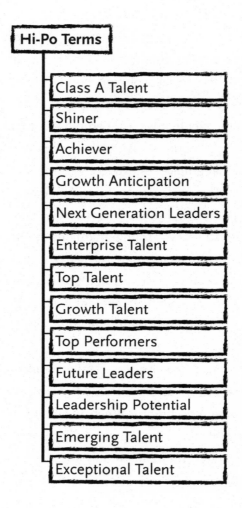

Hi-Po Terms

- Class A Talent
- Shiner
- Achiever
- Growth Anticipation
- Next Generation Leaders
- Enterprise Talent
- Top Talent
- Growth Talent
- Top Performers
- Future Leaders
- Leadership Potential
- Emerging Talent
- Exceptional Talent

Whether you call it HiPos (high potentials), HighPros (high promotability), LoGoes (low potential going nowhere) or use a "nine-box grid" to determine critical or key talent, it's likely that you have a certain vocabulary in your SLOW process to determine who you want to promote, spend money on, keep in position or help to find rosier pastures elsewhere. High potential employees already know they're high potential, so they're probably managing their career daily and not waiting around for something to happen *to* them. We should be asking ourselves more often if it's all really worth the time and effort and if it effectively meets our objective of identifying talent or planning successions. Again, I believe that there must be a better way, yet as Albert Einstein said: "We can't solve problems by using the same kind of thinking we used when we created them."

If I haven't already upset you, and you're still reading, thank you. Again, my point isn't to say that we haven't tried. In fact, many of you may be thinking: *I've been telling my boss this for years!*

Automating SLOP

It's true, many of us have been talking about these processes for a long time but for some reason—be it politics, egos or other priorities—we have only slowly progressed from spreadsheets and PowerPoint presentations to big, heavy IT systems.

Depending on the size of your company, you have probably by now migrated to some species of an Enterprise Resource Planning (ERP) or HR Information System (HRIS) monster. ERP systems materialized in the 1990s and promised to highly integrate and streamline multiple processes and tools throughout the organization. For some companies, they have indeed helped improve processes, provide faster performance analytics and metrics and increase business synergies. So, if ERPs can work for finance, operations and sales, why not for our people dilemma?

Along came the HRIS alternative, with promises to put all our HR data in the same place, so that we could experience the same level of organization that our manufacturing and operational colleagues were already "enjoying." Yes, they were a little ugly and tricky to navigate, but they enabled us to manage multiple processes from the same computer screen. We did, however, continue to have the ongoing struggle with mundane issues like reporting formats and how to get managers to use the system – all taking valuable time and energy away from dealing with the source of the data it eventually spits out.

> ***Software-As-A-Service:*** Software that is rented rather than purchased. Instead of buying software and paying for periodic upgrades, SaaS is subscription based, and all upgrades are provided during the term of the subscription. When the subscription period expires, the software is no longer valid.[1]

Then along comes a brand-new monster: the exponential proliferation of a new species of online mega-creatures like Google, Facebook and LinkedIn. We've quickly grown so accustomed to these interactive giants that we can hardly live without them. With this brave new interconnected realm of social media, users have come to expect attractive, easy to navigate, fun (yes, FUN) and quick (two clicks, no more!) tools to work with every day.

The monster HRIS companies have finally picked up on this and are trying to move rapidly to more interactive systems that resemble our playtime networks. They look nicer and attempt to include collaborative features, but I'm convinced that employees will not be fooled. It will take more believable "what's-in-it-for-me" answers than simply redressing the monster to get employees to take it to the dance.

With all the companies that have systems in place to count their employees, each year spending billions of dollars in the process, the question remains: are companies getting their money's worth? Do they even know how much they're spending? What exactly has been the ROI? If you knew then what social media and SaaS solutions would bring, would you have made the same decision? When I asked Captain Mike Barger, Co-Founder and former

---

[1] *http://www.pcmag.com/encyclopedia*

SVP Field Operations at the American low-cost airline JetBlue Airways about his experience with choosing an HRIS, he had this to say: "The way I like to describe our HRIS experience is that you never stop implementing it, so it's never finished; you're just constantly launching the project. We spent several million dollars because we desperately needed an HRIS of some sort. At the time, all three major vendors we were considering had reputations of being 800-pound-gorilla software programs that once you bought them, they owned you instead of you owning the system. What we ended up choosing was effective but extremely cumbersome, very time-consuming to deal with, difficult to customize and expensive to upgrade. In the end, it was a difficult solution that was not cost-effective. Systems have moved on now, but it's difficult to change when the gorilla is still in the room."

So, let's imagine that your company could greatly reduce its HRIS investment by using a more efficient process for identifying talent that doesn't thrive on complexity, doesn't require a large scale software development investment, actually gives you the data you need and is even a pleasure to use. What if you could trade in the gorilla for a much smaller, tamer animal that's easy to install, simple to use, and if the upgrade isn't good enough, as uncomplicated to delete as an application on your smartphone?

Between Paradigms: The Power of Disruptive Technology

The HR universe is stumbling between paradigms, poised to make a quantum leap in an unprecedented way when doing business. Companies are attempting to be more people-focused, data is easier to enter and consolidate, and collaborative workplaces have begun to disrupt all that we thought we knew. The former processes and systems don't work in the same way that the larger "connected" world works, and the new concepts that have taken off like wildfire in the social media arena haven't quite yet been embraced to their fullest inside organizations. Wrapping our brains around the concept of giving employees more say in crucial matters can be a challenge. Companies exist with certain product and service missions in mind. Shareholders want more return on their investments. Unions are gaining or losing power and influence, depending on where you operate. And employees' expectations about "work" are quite different from not only those of their grandparents and parents but also the expectations of their older siblings.

This conflict between old and new ways of doing things won't be solved anytime soon just by introducing technology. We remain human beings with personal beliefs, values, and histories that aren't always based on a strict logic that could be programmed into a machine or robot. And in organizations, we are forced to contend with power, politics and hierarchical issues.

Since tagging has been around a long time, I won't call it a disruptive technology as such, but tagging *would* be a disruption to the HR function if not viewed as an evolution of the way we've done things in the past. Tagging for talent is absolutely simpler than prior approaches, especially since it takes advantage of behaviors that people are engaging in anyway, if only outside of work.

Cécile Demailly heads up Early Strategies, a Paris-based disruptive change consultancy that helps companies in their approach to early adoption to technology and change. I met with Cécile to find out why companies are so timid about adopting new technologies that can radically change and help their businesses. With more than 20 years of experience in senior international product management and marketing roles at behemoths like IBM, AT&T, and GE, her focus is to bring clients up to speed with the always changing market, align their vision and accordingly enhance their strategies and plans.

"It's often a matter of who has the power in distributing the information," Cécile said. "If it's a hierarchical organization, often the executive team doesn't want a tool that allows people to find and contact each other freely and start working without asking their bosses for information. We are in a world where the talent management role is not unique to HR. It's not just HR's job to enter the skills of everybody into a system and then manage to find people on demand. People have to know themselves, be able to find new people for their teams or projects and be available if there is a request and so on. This can be scary for the hierarchy."

I would go one step further and say that it can also be daunting for employees because it's more than the employee promoting their skills and attributes; it's their peers doing so, as well. The result is a more transparent workforce. Employees' skills, knowledge, attributes, and interests will be more visible throughout the organization. Employees already have the responsibility to be available and make visible the talents that they have to offer the organization. Some employees are quite adept at being visible; for other employees, this visibility can come with connotations as varied as "successful," "brown-noser" or "overly ambitious." Having our peers involved in the process brings disruption not only to HR, of course, but also to employees themselves.

Let's imagine the following scenario: the merger or acquisition comes along, and although we've been forewarned by reading the business school case studies, we're still afraid to fall into the category of "what went wrong" stories. M&A's are always full of surprises that are difficult to uncover in the process and integrating the talent of each company can be a tactical and emotional nightmare. If there were a way to see the entire skill set of the company at a glance based on peer-to-peer identification of talent, you could make better decisions about where to distribute talent, find the needed skills and protect resources that might be vulnerable during the confusion.

Getting back to my earlier point about disruption, we are now in a world where information is available from everywhere to everyone. I see this as a real opportunity to increase trust and transparency in the organization. Some senior executives will also be visionary enough to see the potential. It's obvious that our jobs become a lot easier when we know where to get the right skills or information. Middle management, on the other hand, may see this as a problem because it would mean the information was circulating without it going through them first for validation; and that skills were being uncovered without their knowledge. Cécile acknowledges middle management's fear of losing control: "This transparency of information is changing their role, giving middle managers yet another objective to transform themselves." The leader or manager who encourages transparency will weather the storm much more smoothly, while also having more information about the skill sets they are leading. Employees, in turn, will be more likely to stay with progressive companies that allow them to be recognized for what they can contribute and how well they share their abilities with others.

Successfully transitioning from one HR paradigm to another will require, nevertheless, changes that are even more basic. The importance of this was brought into sharper focus one day while in the early stages of drafting this book. A small glitch in my workday made me conscious of a huge hypocrisy that is happening in organizations insofar as mixed messages being sent to employees about the use of technology. My example would be funny if it weren't so frustrating. I was working temporarily in an office building in the center of Paris and was scheduled to be on a Skype call with a colleague in North America. Suddenly an error message popped up on my laptop screen: "You are not allowed to access this page." Hmmm. I wasn't sure why my Skype access was being blocked. I walked out to the receptionist to ask if there was a problem with the server, or if this was a policy issue with the company that rented the office space. When I approached the receptionist, she didn't look up right away. Being in a bit of a rush (by now I was 10 minutes late in making my appointed phone call), I leaned over the desk to get her attention. The reason why she was otherwise occupied became instantly clear. Apparently, I was interrupting a very important Facebook chat session. I couldn't make an international call to conduct business on

Skype because my access was blocked, but she could instantly pull up her Facebook and chat with friends about personal stuff. I thought: *Something's wrong with this picture!*

Tagging: A Return on Investment

There seems to be a lot of pressure on HR people to demonstrate a solid ROI on any social networking initiative, but I am confident that once companies can navigate through the "disruptive" phase, the personal and financial return on investment of using the masses to help improve a company's profitability will be enormous. The most obvious are that the HR function immediately becomes more robust and effective. Say, for example, that you work in an organization of 10,000 employees, and the generally recognized assumption is that there is one HR person for every 100 employees – or 100 people working in HR. Let's assume that half of them (which we know isn't true) are working on talent development, acquisition, and recruitment. What if you could instantly add 9,900 people to help with these processes, with no increase in the company's payroll? That's the power of tagging.

If you are skeptical about the value of multiplying your talent identification resources to include all employees, I'd like to ask you to complete just half of the following list. It doesn't have to be perfect, and you can even estimate low. My guess is that the cost of tagging for talent will still be significantly less than the value that you assign to any single item on this list.

Factor	Cost?
Person(s) managing internal recruitment	
Time to identify an internal candidate	
Time to find the new person's replacement	
Time to get the new person up to speed	

Training new employee	
Time the job is open and work not being done (productivity)	
Temporary resource(s) to fill the job while it is vacant	
Recruiting fees, advertising, internal job boards	
Pre-assessment tools or process	
Preparing and presenting SLOW or SLOP	
Other	
TOTAL	

Welcome to the Tagosphere

It's about time that we begin to look at a workplace that combines the talent management skills of Human Resources and the expertise of managers with the eyes and ears of the entire employee population. If we can harness the collective intelligence of people to design massive infrastructure projects, transport people around the globe in high-tech jets, and serve the same quality of coffee or hamburger with the same level of service no matter where you might be in the world, then certainly we can take the necessary steps to find, recognize and promote talent more efficiently.

So, welcome to the Tagosphere, where I'm going to show you how you can make an enormous difference in your business, your life and the lives of your colleagues. In the following chapters, I will cover five key concepts of tagging for talent:

Tagability: *Here we will review the basic "how" and "what" to tag, the simplicity of the process and how peers can help identify hidden talent.*

Tagitude*: How tagging with transparency will help to create an attitude of trust and support.*

Tagutation*: How the self-regulating aspect of tags ensures their quality and helps employees build, monitor and protect their personal reputations.*

Tagognition: *Why peer-to-peer tagging is one of the easiest ways to foster employee recognition, something that is in short supply in organizations today.*

Tag Time: *Why opportunities to tag are endless and bring with them many rewards.*

Throughout these chapters, the two "main characters" will make their appearance to help us understand both viewpoints and how the two can come together for a common cause of finding hidden talent within an organization.

So, are you ready to put all of this HR talk about finding and retaining talent into the hands of your employees? Trust me on this: Everyone—not just HR—can determine who is good at what, if given a way to express it. Whether you're the anTAGonist on the fence or the early adopter proTAGonist, allow yourself to be provoked, challenged and hopefully inspired as you go boldly into the Tagosphere.

TAGABILITY

CHAPTER 2

/tagability/ *verb*/*adjective*. the roles, knowledge and behavior strengths we observe in our colleagues and ourselves.

Think of one or two people with whom you work closely. These colleagues don't necessarily have to be on your team or even in the same city, but you interact enough to know them fairly well. You might see them every day, or only have monthly project meetings via telephone or video conference. If you had to come up with five words to describe what they're really good at, what would those words be? Would you identify skills related to their job functions? Are they great in marketing, finance or engineering? What about *how* they perform their work: are they efficient, creative, technical or precise? What about things you've learned or noticed about them over time that may seem completely unrelated to the job they do, such as being artistic, articulate, insightful or humorous?

Now for a really important question: Have you ever shared with these people any of the positive things that you've noticed? If you have, bravo! Unfortunately, many of us don't take the time or find enough opportunities to do so. Depending on your cultural or personal background, you might be embarrassed to give a compliment. In fact, you may not even particularly like them other than for the attributes they bring to your projects or daily work requirements, so why bother going out of your way to tell them something good? Now imagine a workplace where your colleagues and peers could identify *your* talents, maybe even some that you didn't even realize are valued because they come naturally to you. What impact do you think this would have on your job performance, motivation and future potential? How do you think this might change the course of your day, project and career?

The very nature of the Tagosphere gives us the opportunity to create opportunities for what I call "Tagability," or the means to identify and be identified for positive attributes, skills, and competencies – some of which are evident and others that are more obscure. Tagability can be nothing short of transformational for a person's career, as it gives a fuller perspective on any given individual. I'm thinking now of my friend Bruno, who has many obvious talents. His business card notes that he is a Ph.D. and research fellow working for the leading beauty and cosmetics firm L'Oréal with expertise in hair biology – all very impressive. Yet equally impressive are Bruno's attributes that are not displayed on his business card. He has lived, traveled and worked all over the world. His career spans more than 35 years in many specialized fields, including embryology, glycans biology and functions, skin pathology, retinoids pharmacology, skin, and hair follicle stem cells, and *in vitro* reconstructed skin. Bruno's scientific knowledge has made him a recognized international expert in his field and unique in the global cosmetics industry. He has taught at renowned universities around the world and sits on a number of prestigious boards.

But that's not all! Bruno is proficient at sailing, collects antique cameras, admires modern art and is a fan of aeronautics. When I asked him how these seemingly unrelated talents translate to his work as a scientist, he said this: "In my job it's important to see the world through different lenses, with the eyes of a biologist *and* philosopher, and with concepts that can be applied to any organized 'society'—whether it's a group of cells or tissues or a team of individuals.

Bruno has even performed a "one man show" at a Paris theater entitled: "The Wisdom of Hair." Clearly, there's no way that Bruno's business card or job title could capture his multifaceted experience (can yours?) but all of this could be brought to light in the Tagosphere.

Tagability is not about our emotional relationship to an individual; rather, it's a way for us to draw out other people's observable attributes into bits of information that will help them (and us, as colleagues) have a much more gratifying and productive workplace experience. Before you doubt the power of small pieces of information to affect positive change for the greater good, consider the CAPTCHA technology developed at Carnegie Mellon University. CAPTCHA – an acronym for Completely Automated Public Turing test to tell Computers and Humans Apart – is the distorted words and numbers that some websites make you retype to verify that you are a real person before you can post a comment, send an email or purchase a ticket. "The little puzzles work because computers are not as good as humans at reading distorted text," says Luis von Ahn, a CMU professor who was part of the CAPTCHA team. Luis and his colleagues hypothesized that with millions of people already entering words every day to confirm their identity, wouldn't it be great if they could "capture" some of the data from millions of individuals and apply it to a good cause?

They decided to get the world, literally, to help digitize documents like old paper books and ancient manuscripts through a program cleverly called reCAPTCHA. Here's how it works: After a computer has finished scanning, digitizing and converting manuscripts into words, there is a natural fall-out of text that the computer hasn't been able to convert. This is where Von Ahn's idea comes into play. Today, each time you enter these security verification words, there are now very often two words to enter instead of one. You may get cleared by the security program for only one of the words; the other goes into a gigantic database. After a statistically significant number of people have typed the same thing for these images, the fall-out text is accepted as the most likely interpretation. (Yes, even computers need human beings to finish their work!) So while millions of people around the world are ensuring the security of their credit cards, they are also contributing to the digitalization of ancient manuscripts or classic literature. Now, tagging in the workplace may not result in huge altruistic outcomes for humanity, but it does put into perspective how simple it can be to get employees to identify people's talents in a global workplace collectively. Why leave it up to one or two managers or a small group of HR professionals to do this massive job for an entire company when the entire company can do it for the good of all?

Tagability in Action: How and What to Tag

TAG ME!

Let's start with you. Do you remember the interview process that you went through to get your current position or one of your past jobs? Even those of us who recruit people every day have, at some point, been on the other side of the desk. There was, of course, your smartly formatted resume neatly listing your previous experiences and accomplishments. Maybe you found your current employer (or they found you) through a headhunter, in which case there were reference checks and maybe even an assessment of some sort. You may have interviewed with several people within a company, answering their questions to satisfy any doubts or ensure that you had the right experience and skills to fill the role. Then one day, you got the call: YOU had been selected for the position and, by the way, were you able to start first thing Monday morning?

In many companies, this is where your past ends. Sure, your work experience might be entered into a database somewhere but, frankly, most employers have just spent so much time and money to find and research everything about you that now they just want you to get to work. So the new hire orientation begins; you know, where organizations do their best to bring you up to speed on the *company's* history, or "how we do things here" and other processes that you'll need to understand in order to have a successful career.

Imagine that you could quickly capture the talents a new hire is bringing and not let them be forgotten the first day of the job. I'm not talking about a self-service competency database or automated resume scanning software. It's a very simple exercise that employees can enter themselves—not just in their first weeks of the job but anytime going forward.

To do so, you first go into a simple application, either on the company's Intranet or on your mobile device and select "Tag Me." Here you have the opportunity to enter keywords that best describe what YOU think you're good at in three easy categories:

Roles / Jobs

This is where you would tag the various roles or jobs in which *you* feel that you exhibit particular talents. Try not to think of this just in terms of your job title; you can be a Vice President of Marketing but demonstrate talent as a coach, speaker, teacher, manager, expert or consultant. Remember, tags are simple. The best Tags are one-word descriptors, two maximum. What roles or job tags would you give yourself right now?

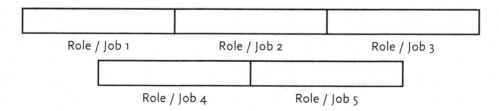

Knowledge / Skills / Expertise

Now you have the opportunity to list the skills or knowledge areas in which you feel you excel or have a particular expertise. A complete list of possible attributes would fill up an entire book, so I won't list them here; however, it's worth elaborating on a few examples to demonstrate the endless possibilities. Some of your skills could be directly related to your current job. Let's say you're a software engineer. You might have certain programming language expertise such as PL/SQL, C-Sharp or HTML. You might indicate innovation is a skill through the patents you've been awarded for inventions you've designed.

Other knowledge, skills or expertise may not be directly job-related. You may have developed sales skills because you learned them by selling Avon or Amway, or back in high school, you sold the most candy bars to raise money for that senior year band trip to Disney World. You've become an expert in change management (you've relocated umpteen times as a child because your mother or father was in the military) or negotiation (you're the parent of three teenagers). You may possess some language abilities you learned from your Japanese ancestors, or during an expat assignment you picked up a good level of Spanish, or those online courses have helped you become conversational in Portuguese. Tag them all!

What three to five pieces of knowledge, skills or expert talents do you possess that you would list immediately?

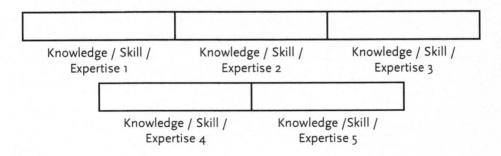

Knowledge / Skill / Expertise 1	Knowledge / Skill / Expertise 2	Knowledge / Skill / Expertise 3

Knowledge / Skill / Expertise 4	Knowledge /Skill / Expertise 5

Personal Skills / Values

Finally (and probably more tricky to define) are the personal attributes and values that make us unique as individuals and further define who we are. Whether learned on or off the job, you might have a particular expertise in soft skills, like listening because you've been volunteering at a local grief-counseling center, or you're known for your "composure," even in the most heated meetings with customers. Do you consider yourself to be creative? Honest? Reliable? Kind? Organized? Adaptable? Tolerant? Observant? Compassionate? Which three-to-five personal skills or values would rise to the top of your list?

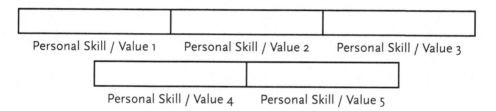

Personal Skill / Value 1	Personal Skill / Value 2	Personal Skill / Value 3

Personal Skill / Value 4	Personal Skill / Value 5

That's basically it! Well not entirely, but we'll cover how to use these self-perceptions a little later. As you take the time to reflect, you can return to these pages and add or delete tags, making a note of your roles, job skills, and soft skills, as well as your personal attributes and values.

TAG OTHERS!

This is where the exercise that you just did becomes even more interesting. I know you're interested in what you think about yourself, but are you also curious to see whether others have identified the same skills, expertise, personal attributes and values in you as you have? Or have they noticed other things about you that you take for granted or don't realize you're good at? In which context, role or job do others see you demonstrating these strengths? And if we turn this around, what do you notice about your colleagues, managers and team members that they may not see?

Tagging others works the same way as tagging yourself. Is there a co-worker in whom you have observed a skill, expertise or personal attribute that you appreciate? Write down one or two words that identify the person's talents, following the same logic you did for yourself above. These qualities may exhibit themselves very explicitly at work, or they may appear in a variety of circumstances when you interact with the person on the job. Don't be shy about choosing your own words to describe the talents instead of picking them out of a box. (We'll cover when and where to tag a little later in the Tag Time chapter.)

So you begin tagging others, and they respond in kind, but what about those employees who don't get tagged? The ideal scenario is that these individuals will figure this out themselves and begin tagging others – which in turn, will lead to others tagging them. If the employees don't notice a lack of tags, it might take a little coaching by a manager, peers or HR. However, once they see the benefits of being more visible, they will begin reaping the benefits of the Tagosphere. Another response to not being tagged is that these employees remain disengaged from the process, either because they may not have the same level of need for feedback as others or because they might just see themselves as too busy to participate. In this case, the downside isn't so much for the individual as it is for their peers, who will miss chances to be tagged by these individuals. Another possible reaction could be that some employees see all of this "helping each other out" as silly, nonsensical and even manipulative. Realistically speaking, not everyone will see the benefits of tagging or be ready to adopt a new practice right away, but hopefully, through their peers, they will be encouraged to share their talents more willingly. When the next job goes to the person whose hidden talents have now become more apparent, the reluctant individuals may reconsider.

Those of you who have thought ahead are probably wondering, *What if somebody tags me with things that I don't agree with?* What happens next is a bit like getting those Argyle socks as a birthday gift from your Aunt Alice. On the one hand, you appreciate her thinking of you every year and taking the time to select (what she thinks) is the perfect gift. On the other hand, you really don't think these gems match your style or personality, so you return them to the store. Your dear Aunt Alice will never find out, anyway.

Receiving a tag you don't want is a bit like those Argyle socks. You can appreciate that somebody noticed something in you that the person thought you would like, but you want to have the opportunity to reject it, too. In the

Tagosphere, everyone is able to self-manage the tags they receive. Unlike the endorsements that you give and receive on networking sites, you have the opportunity to accept or reject tags as they are given, and you are the decision maker of what goes public. The tricky part is for you to decide if, in fact, this is a quality somebody sees in you that you have not recognized in yourself, or if the tag is simply not accurate. To continue our Argyle sock analogy, if Aunt Alice gives you a pair of socks that you don't like but a tie that you adore, you can return one (reject it) and keep the other (accept it); the same applies to tags you receive. Better yet, in the Tagosphere, you don't have to go to the store to return anything!

Here's an example of where rejecting a tag might be appropriate:

William from Shanghai participates in a meeting where Sudha from Mumbai has given a presentation. William thinks to himself, *I had no idea that Sudha spoke Mandarin, and I'm really impressed with her knowledge on the subject of real-time data acquisition.* William later tags Sudha with "presentation skills," "data acquisition" and "Mandarin." Sudha receives these tags and chooses to accept the first two but not the last. She brushed up on a few words of Mandarin for the presentation knowing that some of the participants would be pleased that she was well prepared, but she does not consider it a strength at all. Now, what happens if Sudha actually accepts the "Mandarin" tag? No harm is done, and the whole system doesn't get thrown out the window. Again, the beauty of Tagability is that the number of people who tag Sudha with the same talent is what makes the real difference as to the importance each skill or attribute is given. Still, the underlying message that Sudha receives immediately is that her audience (William, in this case) really appreciated the effort she put into her presentation. Going forward, she's more likely to repeat this behavior when preparing for other presentations. Sudha will not only continue developing herself but has also helped to create a positive work environment in the process.

Tagging Competencies: Bringing Them to Life

Competency management has always mystified me. Can anyone really "manage" competencies? We can decide what skills and behaviors we'd like to see more of in a company, yet managing them is next to impossible.

Like SLOP, the value is often at the part of the process where managers get together and mutually decide which competencies are important. If this were the only thing they had to do in their jobs, they'd be more than pleased to help out. But the time it takes to agree on the definitions, content makeup and even the titles of the competencies can often be slower than evolving business needs and changing customer requests. So, we carry on designing competency matrices and the associated recruiting guidelines and training plans to ensure that this hard work pays off, that is, until the competencies we've developed need to be changed or modified, and then it starts all over again.

There are positives, points out Hilary Ellis, an expert on competency development at Arle, a private equity partnership. "All companies need a common understanding or vocabulary to work from. The same word can mean different things to different people, but in the context of a company, these words mean *specific* things. Defining competencies clearly gives us a common language, so that when we say that we want to improve our entrepreneurship, for example, we all know that we're talking about the same thing. This helps to avoid misunderstandings and disagreements down the road when we talk about strengths, development needs, career moves and who we should hire by providing criteria that are observable and objective."

Hilary and I agree that bringing competencies to life is the bigger issue. Competencies are not just something stagnant sitting in a file somewhere. Like the people they describe, they need to live, breathe, grow and make an impact. Any manager brave enough to go against the political grain will tell you that the time and effort put into designing, evaluating, agreeing upon, then redesigning competencies is often lost on the perceived value they bring later.

Tagability has a heartbeat. By allowing employees to Tag the talents of their peers through mass collaboration, what is likely to emerge is an ever evolving and more pertinent list of competencies. Matched with the company's already predefined list of key knowledge, skills, and behaviors, it creates a clearer vision of organizational intelligence and capabilities. With more relevant data to work with, we can dedicate more time to developing and nurturing our teams.

As an example, wouldn't it be great if we could allocate more time to coaching—something that we complain leaders don't do enough of? (That's right, they're in their offices filling in spreadsheets!) This coaching time can be used to address, among many other things, questions that the employee may have as a result of the tags they've received or concerns about those they haven't. The coaching conversation is bound to be more personalized and probably more applicable to what's going on in the employee's work life.

Johari Window[2]

	Known to self	Not known to self
Known to others	*Arena*	*Blind Spot*
Not Known to Others	*Façade*	*Unknown*

---

[2] *"Johari Window" by w: User: Simon Shek http://en.wikipedia.org/wiki/Image:Johari_ Window.PNG. Licensed under Public Domain via Commons - https://commons. wikimedia.org/wiki/File:Johari_Window.PNG#/media/File:Johari_Window.PNG*

Similar to Luft and Ingham's Johari window, the ability to identify differences in perception is another advantage provided by Tagability. Competencies you see versus what others see may not always be the same, and this provides a number of assessment and self- development opportunities. Look back at the list of talents that you've tagged yourself with. Would your peers tag you with the same talents? As an IT expert, you may have given yourself some tags around strategy, vision or marketing but do your peers see these same attributes? If not, why? Do you make them visible at work? Would you like your colleagues—or better yet, the boss—to see these talents? If so, what can you do to make these talents more visible? If you've tagged yourself as "leader," but your peers see you as an "expert," is there a message to be taken away? This creates an excellent opportunity for HR and managers to play a greater role in helping employees identify the projects, tasks or jobs that will bring these talents out and make them more visible. Also, it will assist managers in positioning their staff in roles in which they will excel versus placing them in roles that do not play to their strengths. Likewise, "frustrated talents," or those employees who have unknown or underutilized capabilities, can be identified and recognized before it's too late.

When employees feel that their skills are being understood and considered by management, it's good for business. Are your employees' strengths best positioned to respond to your customers' demands? By way of example, one day I was talking with Deb, a consumer affairs coordinator for the pet food division of a major American food company. She told me that she is required to analyze trends and compile monthly summary reports of business drivers based on calls to the company's hotline – some 5,000 calls per week. "I told my boss that she's not using me to the best of my ability," Deb explained. "I said that everyone knows I'm really good at speaking to upset consumers. That day, I'd taken an escalated call from one of our phone representatives. The pet owner had called in about a change in the company's cat food recipe—uh, the recipe had changed five years ago

—but this man was worried because his cat was moving around much more slowly and he thought it might be due to the recipe change. After learning that Felix was 18 years old and making the customer aware that the recipe hadn't changed recently, *we* were able to conclude that Felix's advancing age was probably responsible for his slowing down."

After speaking up, Deb was able to enlighten her manager about her skills in dealing with difficult customers, and she was able to handle all such calls going forward, as well as training representatives in how to handle the more sensitive calls before they escalated. Deb's manager didn't lose power by knowing her team member's strengths; if anything, the department (and their customers) benefited. If Deb hadn't spoken up to her boss, how much longer would her abilities have gone unnoticed? Tagging gives employees a "voice" and managers the power to address employee needs earlier, rather than waiting for the employee to leave the company to work for a competitor. If given the opportunity, Deb could have quickly and easily tagged herself as "compassionate," "calm," "diplomatic," "conflict management" and "problem solver."

Using Tagability to Support People Processes

All of this "saying something good about yourself and others" seems to have merit besides being warm and fuzzy, but how can you get the maximum out of it to support your current people processes or better yet, *improve* them? The link with competencies is similar between these processes and the tagging concept, but Tagability goes far beyond competency management.

Succession Planning

We know from our earlier "CEO in the helicopter" example that it's impossible to see all of our talents from above, no matter how great the view. If you now reflect on the impact of employees lending their eyes and ears to help identify talent that they see every day, the succession planning and talent identification process becomes a whole lot richer. Your company may call the process Talent Review, Succession Planning, People Review or something similar. If you're an HR professional or manager of a team, you probably know the drill all too well. If you're an employee not directly involved in this process, you may have never even heard of it. In addition to the "high potential" and other identifiers already mentioned, companies generally have various categories of succession or talent that look similar to these:

Prepared Successors – Qualified Successors – Ready Now Successors
Future Potential – Pipeline Candidates – Promotable Now
Promotable in One to Two Years – Promotable in Three to Five Years
Emergency / Temporary Replacements – Potential Senior Executives
and more

It's generally a list of people put together from the bottom up, suggested by each manager and based on a variety of "data" such as performance, competencies, seniority, expertise and so on. It all sounds very organized and thought out, and in many companies, well managed and accepted. The information flows up the chain and culminates in a review of some sort.

A typical example might go something like this:

A group of your executives is sitting in a conference room at the corporate headquarters after having the "Talent Review" on their calendars for six months now. (If you hadn't scheduled them so far in advance, they'd be too busy to be there.) They know it's that time of year to review and talk about all the high potential candidates and experts at risk for leaving. The person chairing the meeting, usually somebody from HR, welcomes everyone and the slides go up.

Over the course of a few hours—if lucky, we get the execs for a whole day—they discuss the key people who keep the organization running. During the meeting, we learn about people like Richard, whose sales achievements helped the company meet its financial objectives or the service department that will be reorganized in the coming months. We also see a lot of "re-gifting" going on—you know, last year's rising star has suddenly been made available by her manager. We also hear some highly stimulating and purely data-driven assessments such as:

"He's a nice guy. I saw him do a presentation once and he was really good."
"I don't think she'll move. She just got married to Mark in Accounting."
"I met him during a leadership class in Chicago, and he seemed bright."

In reality, at the very senior level, the CEO probably doesn't need a meeting to know his "Top 50." The opportunities to meet these leaders are much more frequent than meeting those further down the organization chart. Even though having discussions about our people is valuable, it may be limited to obsolete data or circumstantial references by the time the talent review comes around. When we think about how the list of people is prepared, especially when it originates from deep down in the organization (particularly, in large organizations), it's normal that it has already been narrowed down by the time it gets to the top for review; or, lo and behold, some managers may even intentionally "neglect" to put out (make visible) their people who they fear might be attractive to other departments.

Imagine this same process with current data, based on the observations of many, transparent and not lost within the organization. Since you now understand how and what to tag, you would probably agree that the quality of your succession planning or talent review process would immediately improve and you wouldn't even need to secure a slot on the execs' calendars. You'd have a more rounded view of your people and would be able to place them better according to what you know about them –not just from a protective manager but from everybody. I wouldn't say that we need to let the top leaders off the hook by throwing the talent review process out of the window, but this modern approach will provide additional input to better match what the business is seeking and what individuals are looking for.

Practically speaking, many of our career changes have been thanks to, or as a result of, our network relationships. We all know that our networks are quickly expanding due to technology. These days, we build them quicker virtually, but we can't discount the important value of our face-to-face networks—those people we meet at conferences, seminars, through professional associations and such. And given that most of us spend more waking hours at work than at home, it's no surprise that our internal company networks may provide greater insight into many roles and opportunities within the organization.

Finding the next job may likely come from not only our performance results but through a variety of situations. Reflect upon your own career path. Did it come from a formal plan or from relationships you've developed over time inside the company? Maybe you found your position through someone you were introduced to at a company conference, golf outing or business trip. Or perhaps you vetted a new team member while working on a cross-company project or at a training course. So what if we could leverage this peer and network support through the application of tags? Not only would companies find a larger pool of talent previously scattered about, but employees would have greater visibility of career opportunities. Using the knowledge of networked people has always been valuable, and now tagging makes it searchable.

Performance Management

We've already touched upon performance management; regarding that, let's not forget that objectives are usually communicated from the top—driven by current market conditions, global company initiatives, strategic plans and so forth—and cascaded throughout the organization. The whole point of the objective-setting process is not only to ensure that every employee is rowing in the same direction, but it's also a means used to assess the performance of our teams and provide an outlet for feedback. According to the Corporate Executive Board, daily informal feedback from direct managers can impact engagement capital by up to eight percent; however, it's interesting to note that only 12 percent of managers provide informal feedback at that frequency, and only 50 percent of managers deliver informal feedback more than once a month. If we consider that, according to this research, informal feedback builds more engagement capital when received from peers than from a manager, then peer-to-peer tagging could provide a helpful solution.

But as we know, things certainly aren't static; not only are the dynamics of the company constantly changing, individuals are too. And although the frequency of providing feedback may seem like more than enough to satisfy many managers, employees today expect even more. When employees are not employees—when they're just people at home using apps and websites where getting "likes" and other virtual feedback every day is normal – then why shouldn't they expect the same frequency of feedback within the organization?

Our colleagues see us every day working on projects, dealing with customers, and handling problems and conflicts. They observe us in training courses, presentations, team activities, management situations and operational activities. They see how we handle stress not only when the boss asks for a report at the last minute or when we're summoned to the president's office to explain a project. Denise M. Rousseau, Professor of Organizational Behavior and Public Policy, at the Heinz College and Tepper School of Business at Carnegie Mellon University puts it well: "Who knows better than employees themselves who the contributors are or who is the go-to person with the technical problem?" And with personal situations, such as when the school calls with upsetting news about something your child did that day, when your daughter gets married, or when you've been given a promotion, our peers observe first-hand how we handle, manage, communicate and lead.

Tagability gives employees the opportunity to have a non-threatening performance review every day in a format that's based on a situation, task, action, and result. On top of that, employees won't have to wait for the dreaded review to start seeing where they need to develop and won't be as disappointed when their manager forgets to recognize their accomplishments officially. Of course, when performance review time rolls around, the tag cloud an employee has gathered during the year brings more data again to an otherwise delayed process that often only concentrates on the results of the day-to-day job.

360° Reviews

You may have jumped to the conclusion that peer-to-peer tagging is just like a 360° Review or Assessment. It's true, we do receive a form of feedback with the tags attributed to us by our colleagues, and the idea of using one's tag cloud as a discussion tool with the HR manager or personal coach is similar in some ways to what companies do in a much more formal fashion when they launch 360° evaluation initiatives or assessments. The intention is good, and often the feedback process is rewarding to the individual, yet several hiccups remain with 360° initiatives, in particular.

The first is that the 360° Review is usually offered to a limited number of employees in the organization. Several reasons exist for this, such as the cost of the tool and the time it takes to implement. But more importantly, the usual 360° Review requires a professional, a coach or other certified personnel, to accompany the feedback process – especially when there's a large disconnect or negative outcome as seen by the receiver. Typically, the "high potential" population or even the "problem" population get the majority of time and resources dedicated for this type of assessment. Most companies outsource this process to experts in the field, bringing objectivity to the process or handing off the responsibility to outsiders to validate what we may have already surmised. It comes at a high cost, but we're willing to pay the money to get broader feedback, as the name implies, than from just one manager.

Many learning and development professionals have tried to meet this need for assessing the softer skills by integrating some type of 360° Review or exercise into their classroom curricula or within their Assessment Center or Development Center initiatives. By doing so, more employees are given access to this powerful evaluation instrument, and course feedback suggests that they appreciate the value it brings.

The second issue (and for me, the larger one) is that the 360° Review really only takes a snapshot of an employee's current state and is limited to the number of feedback points, or individuals rating the employee has. These are typically one-off initiatives that might be repeated a few years later with yet another population of reviewers—that is if the employee is still with the organization. One could argue that tagging is also a snapshot approach but, in fact, it becomes more like a motion picture, with the "story" of the employee unfolding over time. Every day, individuals have the opportunity to be noticed and tagged by an unlimited number of contributors and a variety of people they come into contact with. Added together over the course of weeks, months and years, we get a better, more comprehensive view of that person. For the anTAGonists who may be thinking that this undermines the quality of the feedback or the HR manager's role, think again. I'm not suggesting that you throw your 360° or other psychometric testing off of Freud's sofa, but having many more opportunities to discuss feedback with an employee actually makes the coach's or HR professional's role even more valuable, precise and realistic. The employee was involved in the entire process, has validated the tags and has already begun self-assessing what these tags mean. When it comes to coaching time, employees are more open minded about suggestions and actions they can take for improvement. Tagability gives us a more realistic view of ourselves, our teams and our group potential as a company.

Learning & Development Plans

Spending money on development gaps may not always be the best way to improve either ourselves or the capacity of a company's workforce. This particular subject, about "how we spend our lives trying to repair these flaws, while our strengths lie dormant and neglected" is covered in depth in Marcus Buckingham and Donald O. Clifton's book *Now, Discover Your Strengths*. We shouldn't stop helping people improve, but we spend a lot of time and money on creating learning and development plans that may actually be attempting to put square pegs into round holes or trying to "fix" something that can't or doesn't need to be fixed.

Just like with finding the right person for the right job, the results of tagability can help us to target the right people for the right training better. Tagability allows us to discover employees' strengths, as seen by their peers, which can be capitalized on—from both a financial point of view and a knowledge-sharing perspective. If used widely, we'll start to discover a company full of knowledge (tags) that we didn't know we had. Instead of blindly going off and creating the latest and greatest training program around negotiation skills based on some data from last year's development plan and a hunch, we may find that the people who are on the list to attend the future three-day course are, in fact, already good at negotiating. It may not be "negotiations" we're looking to improve but "closing the deal" that's more important.

Similarly, you might just find people within your own organization who are capable of sharing their knowledge and expertise because, on top of their job title or role, they have been identified by their peers as having a particular ability or talent. Let me give you another example in which having peers capture talent would bring big rewards.

A few years ago, while developing and rolling out a global change initiative at an international industrial manufacturing firm with 25,000 employees, it was evident from the beginning that senior leadership involvement would be key to making it work. To accomplish this, the HR SVP (our organizational development consultant) and I insisted at the time on a deployment plan that paired business leaders with HR managers to deliver the program autonomously around the world. However, these people would need to be trained. So we spent months bringing people up to speed. We taught them to change theories and presentation skills, as well as how to deal with different nightmare scenarios to prepare them for what to do if that worst-case situation came up that inexperienced facilitators fear the most. We even gave it a snazzy name: Ways of Working, or WOW.

Over the course of the following year, nearly every employee in the organization had successfully been through a change program of some sort, trained by their peers. You know how the story ends: A new boss comes in after the former one is fired; the HR manager gets fired for being too close to the former boss – which, of course, leads to reorganization, a new name for a new change program, and so on (the fallout from change fatigue is another book entirely).

Now let's fast forward 10 years when all of those internal trainers and facilitators who remained in the organization are now in different jobs, divisions, countries, and levels in the company. They've all shared a common experience, and the competencies they developed during this change deployment (facilitation, listening, planning, teaching, change, etc.,) are nowhere to be found in the company's giant HR system. If the company is looking for someone with facilitation skills, we have to "ask around." If lucky, somebody will suggest: "Hey, you should call Sue White, I think she's done that kind of thing before." Instead, when the need arises again, we'll labor through this entire training process with the same vigor as the first time. Only one thing will be different: 10 years later it will be even more expensive than the first time around. Had Tagging for Talent existed back then, the company could have looked for the needed skills and deployed the new change program much quicker. In fact, by tapping into the experience of its talented people, the company could have altogether avoided the pitfalls of history, reduced the cost of training, and kept its eye on the customer!

When considering all of the above, Tagability starts to make sense in terms of how something as uncomplicated as a thoughtfully considered set of words can greatly benefit both individuals and their companies. It's a daily concept, not a program. It compliments our current processes instead of replacing them. It empowers everyone in the organization, not just a few.

For you, HR professionals out there, fear not. I'm a firm believer that your role becomes ever more critical if this talk about peer-to-peer collaboration is to work. Your expertise is about much more than managing the processes themselves unless that's where you see your strengths. Building coalitions during this type of strategic change are where you shine and create true value for both the organization and its people. Matching talent (fit, mobility, availability, and potential) becomes even more important as speed ensures a greater customer value proposition and having, at your fingertips, a larger, qualified candidate list means more time to contemplate, integrate and innovate.

Putting Tagability into action, however, requires a bit more understanding of the nuances that can ensure its success. Is your organization one of trust or one of power? Do people share willingly or hide knowledge? Does your competition know your employees better than you? What we'll explore next is how the Tagosphere can help begin to break through some of these challenges. Just as Dorothy may have had good intentions in traveling to Oz to find what she was seeking—only to learn that she didn't need to look any further than her own backyard—the answers to some of these questions may be right under our noses. Companies might take a nod from Dorothy's lesson that we don't need to follow the yellow brick road to find the talent hidden right within our ranks. Similarly to how Dorothy's new perspective transformed how she saw things, to fully embrace the power of the Tagosphere, we must also develop what we'll discover next: The magic of Tagitude.

TAGITUDE

CHAPTER 3

/tagitude/ *noun*. transparent and positive identification of talent.

S he unfriended me. Get my WhatsApp? I just tried to FaceTime you. He re-pinned my pin. Let's Skype about it. Hit me up on Snapchat. My tweet has been re-tweeted 300 times. Did you see her post on Reddit? Follow me. Kik me babe. Did you see his selfie on Instagram? He's got 7,000 followers on his YouTube channel. I keep getting added on Google+... ROFLMAO.

Such is the language of today. (If you think the above jargon looks like gibberish, ask any teenager for further explanation.) Time is accelerating in the world of communication. I can still remember the feeling of awe the first time I used a fax machine years ago—like I was Scotty on *Star Trek*, teleporting encrypted text and images through thin air and having it reassemble and print somewhere on the other side of the planet. Technological advances such as facsimile, email, car phones and dial-up modems seemed to have satiated our need for speed. But today, with satellites merging mobility with proximity, our *greed* for speed is voracious. Instant isn't quick enough—or good enough, if our mode of communication isn't *fun*.

As technology continues to infiltrate our lives, there remains little doubt that it is radically changing the way we connect. Online social networks are truly a global phenomenon and, as a result, the intricacies of individuals' public and private lives have become more accessible. Like it or not, everything is becoming more visible to everyone everywhere. Transparency is no longer wishful thinking but rather a key component of "interrelating" that begets both opportunities and challenges. Businesses are increasingly compelled to be more transparent with their financial reporting, interactions with customers and suppliers, environmental impact disclosure, salary and grading policies, just to name a few. In our personal lives, our friends, family and coworkers see what we post online, recruiters look into our backgrounds and experience, governments closely follow (and even fear) what might go viral, the details of celebrities' lives are tracked 24/7 by millions, and even our ex-partners can spy on our activities with amusement or jealousy.

This transparency also applies especially in the Tagosphere. In fact, for the Tagosphere to reach its inherent potential, transparency and trust are essential ingredients. For this reason, allow me to be frank in saying that employees and managers will need to adopt a mindset that is open and encouraging, and be willing to help create an environment where everyone is free to identify and express the strengths they see in themselves and others. At a minimum, this is the foundation upon which the Tagosphere's success is built. Above that, it requires support at the top levels; managers will need to encourage tagging, realizing that ultimately this benefits not just their teams but the business.

All of this may seem frightening or unachievable at first, but tagging for talent makes doing so fathomable. For once, it's an obvious win-win Web 2.0

initiative that goes beyond the collaborative promises. It does require one guiding principle: having the right attitude – or, more accurately, Tagitude.

Tagitude is more than putting in place a tagging system and expecting it to work, especially if today your company doesn't foster a culture of trust and transparency very easily. As we'll see, the entrenched structure of hierarchy, power, job roles and traditional barriers that exist in some companies may seem insurmountable at first; yet with the right Tagitude, you'll see that everyone in the organization has a vested interest in making it work, even at the top. "Corporations need to introduce methods that enable people everywhere in the organization to utilize their individual creative and emotional potential to the fullest."[3] "Yet, at the same time, organizations must also take measures ensuring that individual freedom is combined with an ability to take collective action. Me and we need to co-exist."

You may have come across the term "crowdsourcing" or may even be taking part in this movement with or without realizing it (such as ReCAPTCHA, mentioned earlier). The term "crowdsourcing" has only been around since 2006 (it was coined by journalist and author Jeff Howe), but one can safely say that the activity of many people helping to accomplish a task or group of tasks has been happening for much longer. Think of Habitat for Humanity International. Since its founding in 1976, this nonprofit has organized volunteers and needy families to work together to build 500,000 simple, decent and affordable houses for more than 1.75 million people in more than 3,000 communities worldwide. I'm sure you can think of many other examples of crowdsourcing in the non-virtual world. The Internet has simply made working together on a challenge or project like Habitat for Humanity more global and faster, and the range of projects much vaster.

In *Getting Results from Crowds: The Definitive Guide to Using Crowdsourcing to Grow Your Business*, Ross Dawson and Steve Bynghall

---

[3] *Jonas Ridderstrale, Mark Wilcox, Re-energizing the Corporation: How Leaders Make Change Happen. Jossey-Bass; 1 edition (April 28, 2008) Pgs. 65 and 70*

identify 22 categories of platforms and tools that help tap the power of crowds. "We have entered a new era in which organizations are able to tap the extraordinary power of crowds of people located all over the planet," the authors say. "Implicit in the idea of crowdsourcing is the ability to create value that transcends individual contributions, crystallizing collective insights through structured aggregation." You may recognize some of the 22 categories and not others, but the fact remains that this collaborative way of working has not yet been optimized inside companies, particularly when it comes to identifying and managing talent. Crowdsourcing is also a concept that requires various amounts of trust and transparency between its members.

How is it possible for all levels of an organization to adopt a good Tagitude? You (or others within your company) might be thinking that *Tagability is a great idea, but it would never work here.* Practically every department could cite a reason why they don't want to embrace this change: Accounting would say: "We don't have the budget." Communications would say: "Our culture won't support it." HR and Talent Management would say: "We will lose control." Legal would be paranoid about litigation and IT most certainly would balk at needing to adopt yet another application. Please understand that I'm generalizing here, but I'm sure you can easily insert for yourself the naysayer departments and relevant issues within your company.

Different types of crowdsourcing include:[4]

Service marketplaces	Data
Competition markets	Content
Crowdfunding	Content markets
Equity crowdfunding	Crowd design
Microtasks	Crowd process
Innovation prizes	Labor pools
Innovation markets	Managed crowds
Crowd platforms	Crowd ventures
Idea management	Citizen engagement
Prediction markets	Contribution
Knowledge sharing	Science

Tagging will naturally work best where there is a strong sense of trust, a desire to communicate openly, and a willingness to leave some old processes behind and recognize that the workplace is evolving along with the rest of society. The Tagosphere itself encourages all of this by promoting positive feedback in a simple and unintimidating way. In practical terms, having a good Tagitude means that if you are the tagger, you will *naturally* find opportunities to identify strengths and competencies in your peers and co-workers; and likewise, if you are the tagee, you will have the *choice* to accept or reject the tags you receive. But Tagitude is much more than that.

Sure, we've all run into co-workers during our careers who aren't inclined to support others, so we will encounter adversaries who won't have (or be willing to have) a good Tagitude. What's to be done about that? We don't change the rules of the game because of them. Just as every athlete or entertainer knows that an encouraging crowd is more exciting to play for,

---

4 *Ross Dawson, Steve Bynghall, Getting Results from Crowds. Advanced Human Technologies Inc. (December 2, 2011)*

mostly anyone who has been in the workforce would agree that exhibiting kindness, optimism and collaboration towards one's coworkers makes for a more pleasant and productive day on the job.

And yet, as you're reading this, I am sure you have questions and even concerns about how all of this "transparency" will play out in the Tagosphere, as well as doubts about the feasibility of putting such power into the hands of many. I can only emphasize that any fears about the tagging process are mitigated when individuals begin to see the mutual benefits of giving and receiving feedback in a comfortable, non-threatening atmosphere. Again, we know this because we see it in the social media world, where we secretly (or unabashedly) desire to have our status updates noticed and commented on, our pages "liked," our profiles "viewed," our Tweets "re-tweeted" and our favorite items "re-pinned" by as many people as possible.

Even though many companies are going down this route to revitalize their traditional-looking HR systems, I'm not talking about the concept of an "internal Facebook" for your organization. Although there are similarities, employees tagging behaviors is quite different from employees sharing what they had for breakfast that morning or a snapshot of the sunrise they took on their latest beach vacation. Although the Tagosphere is a serious application of certain kinds of behavior one might be used to seeing on social networks, the most obvious being transparency, along with it comes some perceived obstacles when bringing it into the bureaucracy of management structures.

> *"Working in an environment without transparency is like trying to solve a jigsaw puzzle without knowing what the finished picture is supposed to look like."*
>
> **—Vineet Nayar,** Vice Chairman and Joint Managing Director of HCL Technologies, Ltd.
> *Employees First, Customers Second*

Shining a Light on Hidden Talent

Do you have the right Tagitude? Are you tag-cessible? Here's a way to determine if you're on board with this concept: As a manager, imagine that all your people and their talents are exposed to the rest of the company – meaning, your best employees' skills and competencies are visible to the entire organization. As such, these individuals can no longer be hidden from potential poachers (for example, a manager who is looking for those very same skills or competencies) and the best people on your team are basically an open book or a target to be approached for new opportunities.

What are the risks to this? As a friend in London put it to me one day: "Headhunters see my profile online and call me. Why don't talent managers in my own company do the same?"

We've already talked about how talent in today's world is never really hidden. But even more important, as younger generations of leaders rise to management positions, transparency will become less of a sticking point; for many of them, transparency is a given. It's standard protocol on the Internet today to share and, so why should they expect anything different inside the companies they choose to work for?

Bargaining, negotiating and jockeying all appear in an organization when dealing with resources. Lying (hiding details), stealing (poaching people) and cheating (lack of transparency) all come into play when thinking about power in the talent identification and management marketplace. This is why Tagitude will require a shift in behavior. How many times have you heard or even said that your organization doesn't communicate with its employees as well as it should? It's not so uncommon to hear employees complain that they hear news about their company in the media or see that a key executive is leaving the company (or has already left) from an outside source before they hear it on the inside. Employees who feel communicated *with*, not necessarily *to*, feel accepted and part of the team. They stay motivated and are more willing to help find solutions to problems versus enjoying watching the boss flounder. To be fair, the same holds true for managers who don't receive enough communication or feedback from their employees so that they know what the real problems are or when they are doing well. If you happen to work in an organization where transparency is not a strong point, Tagitude can help foster a more open mindset because it organically creates a collaborative environment to provide feedback, in addition to identifying skills, abilities and behaviors.

The Search for Talent: From Paper Job Boards to Human Job Boards

Recently over lunch, my friend Gina took me for a walk down memory lane, recalling her job with a global banking institution some 25 years ago. She shared how "in the old days," job openings in any given department were listed on an actual piece of paper and posted onto a physical bulletin board. She remembered distinctly that there was a designated spot in the upper-right-hand corner, and everyone knew to look there for the weekly or monthly updates. The jobs were simply listed by title and job code, with a sentence or two describing the position and its requirements. To apply, you simply walked over to the HR department with the job title and code, and expressed your desire to be considered for the position. Of course, it didn't hurt if you knew somebody in the department where the job opening was! Like most companies, this bank has long done away with the old bulletin board. Even in more traditional workplaces such as factory environments, the real pathway to career advancement is now through networking and personal connections, both online and face-to-face.

We've certainly progressed since the days of Gina's nostalgic lunchtime tale. HR departments developed personnel requisition forms, then workforce planning processes, and now fancy online systems (not so coincidentally called "job boards") to keep up with the times. But we still have a long way to go. Even as these systems advance in sophistication, finding talent can still be like a fishing expedition. We cast a line with bait hoping to catch the biggest and fastest fish in the sea. What is evident in many cases is that the "best fish" are happily swimming in their part of the ocean and don't always see the tasty morsel of a job opportunity we've tossed their way. And when we do get a bite, we have somehow managed to design an enormous amount of red tape and "who-can-talk-to-who-when" rules that often let the best fish get away. Knowing that waiting too long will certainly starve the department of much-needed resources, managers don't wait for the mandatory 30- to 90-days posting time to expire before casting their nets further and going covertly to their networks to find the people who they want to take the bait.

If why we moved to posting jobs online was to be quicker and more transparent, then isn't tagging just a natural progression? You know by now that searching for skills and other attributes from the tags accumulated by a larger net of people increases the speed of identifying talent or individuals. But more than that, if talent is recognized by our peers, we've moved on from the old adage, "It's not *what* you know but *who* you know" to "It's not what you know, but who *knows* you know," and what *others* know about you, too! So, guess what? Employees have now become the job board.

Not Just a Number

With the right Tagitude, people are much more than just a number. Internal mobility—or, recruitment from within—has proven time and time again to be one of the best ways to retain and motivate employees over the long term. Shifting marketplaces and business footprints often require headcount adjustments and repositioning of resources. If you are like many companies today, you may be finding that your customer base is not necessarily where your manufacturing is located or vice versa. Even if you're not a multi-national or international company, you probably still face issues of changes that require "mobility" of resources, including your people. Moving an operation to China or Brazil may require reassigning or relocating people to similar or even different positions—and some of your people, probably many, could be harboring talent you don't know about —and that is, of course, where tagging can help identify these "hidden" competencies. Tagitude means opening the lines of communication so that these concealed attributes can be readily seen by many, potentially saving jobs and definitely reducing costs.

Looking at external recruitment only, according to the Corporate Executive Board (CEB), only 50 percent of hiring decisions are "win-win," where both the organization and the candidate are confident that they have made the right decision. That's pretty extraordinary when you think about it. We've assessed and guessed and reference checked, and still there is a 50/50 chance that either the candidate or the employer will be dissatisfied with their choice! Then there's the cost. According to CEB, poor selection decisions can cost an organization up to $30 million annually in additional turnover and underperformance cost. In contrast, hires from win-win decisions—in which both the organization and the candidate are confident that they have made the right decision—exhibit more than 20 percent higher performance and engagement and are almost 50 percent more likely to stay with the organization. What's the remedy? CEB states that we can ensure win-win selections by providing better candidate information to hiring managers at key points in the recruiting process, enabling candidates to make an informed decision to join, and actively tracking the quality of hire data to identify underperforming areas and improvement opportunities.

If we link this data and apply the logic inside for internal recruitment and mobility, it seems apparent that the Tagosphere can be of tremendous value. When tags are visible to line managers and HR, the hiring manager gets much more data to work with about a candidate's strengths and potential contributions, and candidates can better assess what is a good fit for their abilities and career aspirations. Managers would be better equipped to work with employees to align roles and jobs more accurately, promote hidden skills, and provide more targeted development, mobility and career actions. And if tagging begins on day one, candidates and employers alike will feel more assured of their selections.

A leader with the right Tagitude will encourage team members to tag their peers and other colleagues in the organization. The more tags a person has, the more beneficial it is to both the employee and the company. Ultimately, everyone—not just a select few—should have a piece of the action and a stake in knowing what talent exists in the company. Getting to the point where that level of transparency is a reality, however, can bring with it resistance and complications along the way. I've seen my share of talent being hidden, potential and promotability codes being downgraded, so that somebody doesn't get snapped up by another business or manager as well as "side conversations" that have led to a sudden response to a hidden job posting. So, I've tried to anticipate what some resistance and perceived challenges might be, and I'd like to address a few of them head on.

Perceived Obstacles to Tagging and How to Overcome Them

If employees are only hearing good things about themselves, they aren't receiving true feedback.

This is a frequent concern I've gleaned from HR but less from line managers. Not surprisingly, it is also something that a few nervous consulting firms who specialize in coaching and assessment feedback have broached with me. It's important to address this question here, as it relates to Tagitude for a variety of reasons.

Firstly, there are other systems in place (like those mentioned previously) to assess weaknesses and correct poor performance. Maybe more importantly, delivering this type of constructive feedback is never easy (even for professionals who do it for a living) and thus needs to be handled in a more sensitive way, not just as a one-word descriptor or remark. Secondly, when colleagues and peers recognize each other's talents, the tags are of a positive nature; after all, we know that we have to work with these people every day. How long do you think the concept of tagging our colleagues would last if we were being subjected to constant negative feedback? Tagitude means having an open and transparent way to share with people what they're good at – what we see in them that stands out, and makes them unique or special. Managers are ultimately the ones responsible for helping people improve where they fall short. To answer any concerns though, it may come as a surprise to discover that thanks to Tagitude, employees DO receive true feedback, but in a unique way. This is one of the most exciting outcomes of peer-to-peer tagging. Employees can begin to see the gaps between what they perceive versus what others perceive as their strengths, simply by seeing the tags they didn't receive.

Let's take the example of Corinne, who has tagged herself as "leader." Over time, when looking at her tag cloud, Corinne notices that she is only receiving "expert" or "manager" tags from her co-workers. In a soft yet meaningful way, this individual can begin to observe that she sees herself having particular skills or behaviors that others do not see. It's one thing to be told this in an uncomfortable performance review, but if given the opportunity to determine for herself where there is a development need, Corinne can take steps to improve or ask for help before it's too late. By collecting and integrating this feedback, the perceived talent gap can then be used immediately by the individual as an impetus to begin demonstrating, performing or communicating in ways that better align with how she wants to be perceived. For the employee's HR manager, it provides a basis for transparent discussions that will lead to better coaching and development actions; "Megan, it is not because you have the job title of vice president that people necessarily view you as a leader."

When I explain this concept to coaching firms, at first they are surprised, but very quickly their eyes light up. One coach even told me, with his door closed: "This would save me a heck of a lot of time getting to the heart of the problem with some of our clients. We could certainly solve some issues more quickly if we started with data like this but..." He trailed off for a few seconds then completed his thought with equal parts caution and sarcasm. "But then... we might have trouble selling our 360° assessment tool we're so proud of."

Employees will get together and tag each other to make themselves look good.

You might be worried about hearing this or a similar conversation in the hallway: "Hey Ricardo, do me a favor and tag me with 'store manager' and I'll tag you as 'buyer,'" Frankly, two employees complimenting each other and finding a way to do something valuable with these compliments is a good thing. "But that makes the data unreliable," you might say. Actually no, it doesn't, and for several reasons. As we've already established, the value of one tag is not equal to the value of receiving the same tag multiple times. Ricardo being tagged as "buyer" by one of his colleagues does not confirm that he is an exceptionally good buyer; however, if Ricardo receives a large number of the tag "buyer," there may be something to it.

Thanks to the transparency of the approach, others will see what tags you give. As we'll see in the next chapter, with your name associated with the tags, you are more likely to tag what you believe to be true, rather than engage in a meaningless system of patting people on the back. There are some other more complicated approaches out there that seek to give prizes, badges and other rewards for saying good things, and here is where I'd challenge their authenticity. These approaches may provide good analytics but if I think I'll win the latest electronic device for the number of pats on the back I give or receive, then how does the company decide if the feedback I've left is genuine or not? Tagging, on the other hand, is its own reward, for both the employee and the company.

We already have a list of competencies specific to our company.

We already talked about bringing competencies to life in Tagability, so I just want to make one point here as it relates to Tagitude. Many companies have developed competency models, systems, assessments and so forth, and there is no doubt that throwing these systems and tools out the window (along with the money spent to develop them) is an unlikely scenario. Depending on their use, we must admit that mixed feelings remain about their accuracy, shelf life and effort-versus-return value.

Some organizations assess employees against a competency model through the hierarchy, and others allow for self and peer assessment. They are usually limited to a manageable number of keywords and definitions for practical reasons. Unfortunately, for time reasons, we often only glance at the definitions and focus on what we think are the important words when evaluating competencies in ourselves and others. Tagging is an ideal way to capture the text in the definitions along with the competency title, and allow peers to assess against them without feeling like they are completing another HR process. Consider tagging as a rolling forecast of talent and not a quarterly exercise. Isn't this what many companies strive to do with their balance sheets?

People will steal my employees.

The number one resistance that individuals have expressed to me about implementing peer-to-peer talent identification in their organization is a fear that people within their own company will steal their talent. Let's consider this: recent reports from Gallup and other researchers into why people leave jobs show that they don't tend to actually leave a *company* but a *manager* they don't like working for. Employees are less easily poached if they have respect for the person they're working for. The caliber of the boss is the primary reason why people stay and also why they quit – rather than a dislike for the job. In fact, the bad-boss syndrome far outweighs any other consideration for why someone jumps ship, including better opportunities elsewhere. Even poor pay and poor work hours combined don't come close.

Okay, now let's resign ourselves to the fact that poaching *does* exist. Imagine, for example, that an employee has had a bad day or week at work. We all have them so it isn't a stretch to comprehend a time when you're not exactly feeling adoration for your boss or others in your department. It's times like these when an employee is more susceptible to being approached about other opportunities (especially if others know that the employee is feeling temporarily disgruntled). At times like this, the grass looks much greener on the other side of the cubicle and a manager from another department might be ready to swoop in and walk the disenchanted employee across the company courtyard to happier pastures. This sort of situation happens every day and even more so in a world where employees are exposed to jobs outside the company through professional social networks. So what happens in such instances? Well, I believe that employees who feel recognized and gratified in their current positions (even though they may have bad days) aren't actively looking for a new job and aren't easily swayed to leave. Employees who are generally satisfied with the job may be running *towards* something better (in the form of a promotion, a bigger paycheck or more perks) but they aren't running *away* from something (or someone, such as an unsavory boss or difficult co-worker).

Sure, even happy employees are interested in career advancement, increased pay and training opportunities—and therefore may be persuaded to take another position either inside or outside of the organization to meet these needs; and even the manager who is supportive and realistic about the career progression desires of his team members will encounter situations where a seemingly satisfied employee is approached about a new opportunity. Poaching is still not the primary issue. If it is viewed by the manager as somebody "stealing" their best employees then I would ask this manager: "Would you rather lose this person to another division or department inside the company or to your competitor?" I've heard it said that just as employees earn their role in the company every day by what they contribute, a company earns the contribution of its employees by what it gives back to them—and, of course, I don't mean just monetarily. But now let's talk about YOU! You're a good manager, even a great one, with a team that loves working with you. You've even been voted "World's Best Boss" and have the coffee mug on your desk to prove it. Still, you might think: *That doesn't stop someone from coming to my team and "stealing" one of my people.* If this happens, the great leader would likely consider it a compliment because it means he's probably developed a strong team; it means he or she has succeeded at being a "great leader" and a lot of money is being made by consultants and training companies to teach people how to be "great" leaders. Meanwhile, consider that Tagitude levels the playing field in many respects because now everyone has an equal chance. In other words, tagging opens up your visibility to talent just as much as it increases a potential poacher's visibility. If you're a forward-thinking manager, you will understand tagging and quickly embrace it because you're already ensuring good career moves and development opportunities for your people. If you're a great leader, you'll be encouraging your people to tag often.

What if deep down you are, admittedly, a bad manager? You never got the coffee mug with praise on it and your team scatters when you even get close to the coffee machine. Even more likely, you've been promoted to a leadership role of some kind because that was the "next step in the career plan" and it may or may not be something you like or are good at. There's still hope! If you find it difficult to motivate your employees and build relationships with them, tagging is a great opportunity to help do that. You may need to build up some trust with your team if you haven't been so successful up until now, but here's a way to get your team to identify the good things they do. If you can encourage them to tag you as well, you may achieve some self-discovery in a positive, non-threatening way.

My employees will take their tag clouds and send them to headhunters or other companies.

You're right! And if you believe they aren't already doing this then I've got some swampland in Florida that I'd like to sell you. While writing this book, I met with all the well-known major executive search firms in addition to many smaller independent consultancies. They all reported basically the same message: LinkedIn and similar sites like Viadeo are their main research springboards today. Sure, personal relationships continue to be essential and some of the traditionalists still use their Rolodex to find candidates, but they all use social networking sites in their selection strategy as a first identification or screening tool. Anne-Marie Ronayne, owner and international HR consultant and search expert Terra Connecta told me how candidates today are very adept at getting their profiles seen by using keywords that can be easily found by search engines. Several recruiters have even abandoned their heavy, sophisticated systems of the past for ubiquitous online options. And get this: some of the large firms who have kept their systems don't even have links between their global affiliates to share! How long do you think this will last when talent is now a free-market commodity?

But finding somebody and hiring them are two different steps whether they're internally sourced or external to the company. For search firms, "Just having a good resume or LinkedIn profile isn't enough to get the job," Anne Marie confirms. "It relies on the recruiter being good enough to ask the right questions. A candidate will often communicate a frustration as to why they want to leave. It's usually linked to a boss or how they weren't able to get the types of positions that they were looking for and promised by the company."

Headhunters have to do their due diligence to better know their candidates; the same holds true internally. The company, however, has the advantage of a rich accumulation of information about employees' performance, career wishes, mobility options and potential that an external recruiter does not have. Tags themselves won't be the silver bullet that stops people from looking outside, but the emotional engagement that Tagitude encourages and supports brings us much closer to a solution. And although the company has an important role to play, Tagitude empowers employees to take development and career decisions into their own hands before seeking solace from an empathetic recruiter.

This gives the competition too much information.

News flash! Your competitors are probably already analyzing your business strategies and resource capabilities. As workers put more information about their lives online through status updates, location check-ins and resume changes, employers are more at risk of competitors watching their every move. It is an understatement to say that the Internet has exponentially increased the efficiency of accessing information. A recent Forrester Research survey of more than 150 companies that monitor social media showed that more than 82 percent said they use this data for competitive intelligence. With good reason: a single insider's Twitter post can be more valuable than a stack of analysts' research. This kind of intelligence has evolved so much it's now called "social listening" and platforms for it are in abundance in the marketplace.

Another news flash! Your employees' tags won't reduce your competitive advantage; they will _improve_ it dramatically. How? You will better know the talent that you have, as well as your capacity to resource projects and meet customer needs in anticipation. This will make your company a force to be reckoned with. Not forgetting that competitive espionage today includes trolling a vast array of online forums and networks to find your best people, the best defense now (and hasn't it always been?) is making sure that your people are fulfilled, which, in turn, increases their chances of loyalty.

All of this is to say that employees and competitors are not going to stop doing what they're doing, but how employees are treated inside a company will be the primary determining factor for their engagement and ethical behavior. As I used to tell my managers, you have to _re_-recruit your employees every day. Tagitude is an excellent way to do this because you get a whole lot more in return.

If I need to terminate an employee, a tag cloud could be used as a means to challenge my decision.

Unfortunately, there comes a time when we as managers have to perform the task that we dread the most: terminating an employee. If this doesn't affect you anymore, then you may want to reconsider your profession. It may happen as the result of downsizing; the company needs to reduce costs or can no longer afford the person. It can occur because the employee is no longer a good match for the company or hasn't performed up to expectations. In some cases, it may be because the employee has done something wrong: the person has stolen, cheated or committed another offense that has resulted in the decision to *let them go elsewhere*. No matter the reason, we prepare our files, check our documentation and try to anticipate any unexpected surprises.

So let's say that a manager needs to terminate someone and the employee confidently responds by whipping out a list of tags demonstrating all of their illustrious talents as seen by their co-workers. Or the employee stomps into your office flaunting his tag cloud in front of you, saying "Look, boss! Here's evidence of my competencies from my own peers!" At this point, a warning sign flashes through the manager's mind—*wrongful discharge claim!*—and he or she fears that the disgruntled employee will file suit.

A company with Tagitude is prepared for this. To be absolutely clear, Tagitude is not a peace, love and happiness drug that creates a euphoria where everybody suddenly gets along. Tagitude is simply the conduit for an increased level of trust and sharing. And just as tagging doesn't guarantee job security, transparency doesn't equal anarchy. Again, tagging doesn't replace current processes; both management and the disgruntled employee are still bound by the company's rules. Besides the fact that many of the systems that employees use inside and outside of the company typically require an agree/disagree acceptance by the user, none of this usurps the company's established HR policies and procedures. The company's terms and conditions should state that the use of peer-to-peer tagging is voluntary. Just as important, with whatever initiatives are put in place, employers are bound by a set of parameters that obligate them to abide by various employment laws and legislation (EEOC, FLSA, NLRB, etc.) and tagging is no different.

In any event, it's quite possible that the talents an employee is tagged with may not coincide with the reasons for the termination; for example, if the person has hundreds of tags saying that he is good at coding Java software, it doesn't mean that he is being let go because he's not good at coding in Java. It could be for other reasons—such as consistently being late for work or not getting along with team members, or simply because the company no longer requires an employee dedicated to this particular task. Remember, having the right Tagitude means that transparency is a reality on a regular basis. Just like with objectives, any discussions about the difference between tags received and job performance should be ongoing. It also means that managers may find that their employees have skills that are better suited elsewhere on the team, in the company or outside and can find ways to resolve these issues before they materialize into one of the above scenarios.

Tags or no tags, it stands to reason that an employee should never be terminated without the manager thinking through the situation and thoroughly documenting the reasons for ending the relationship. In an example of a restructuring program at an insurance company in Chicago, the HR director told me: "If I had a system like tagging in place, I would have been able to find alternative job placements for people when we put in a new IT system. It no longer required the previous competencies of the team and I would have saved tons of money on severance pay, outplacement fees and recruitment costs."

If we give everyone control my power as a leader will be diminished.

If tagging makes our resources an open book, so to speak, then let's get right down to what may be the real underlying concern: power, or more specifically, loss of power. We might think that our ability to maintain control of our teams, their projects, progress and potential, is what defines our status as leaders. This power to mobilize resources is one determinant, but much like the superhero who has to decide how to use his newfound powers (for good versus evil), leaders must do the same. According to Lee G. Bolman and Terrence E. Deal's *Reframing Organizations: Artistry, Choice and Leadership*, power stems from one of the following sources: position (authority); information and expertise; control of rewards; coercive power; alliances and networks; or access and control of agendas. Wherever it materializes, it exists every day in organizations and can't be ignored.

And as social networking and collaborative ways of working bring on new meaning for management, the rules about power have become even more blurred. In Matthew Fraser and Soumitra Dutta's book *Throwing Sheep in the Boardroom: How Online Social Networking Will Transform Your Life, Work and World*, the authors remind us how "Power in hierarchies is often around who gets which resources, how to hide and protect the best people, because it will reflect on how my team does, thus how I do as a manager. Who gets what/who in the case of scarce resources."

The authors astutely examine the issue of status both from an anthropological and social view; where the survival of a group is the predominant motivator, *expertise* is the overwhelming status factor. Said another way, if you're in a sinking ship, would you more likely team up with the sailor who knows the vessel from bow to stern or the purchasing executive who bought the materials to build it?

And here, dear readers, is where we sink or swim. If the person with the expertise is not necessarily the person who holds the executive job title, then this fear of giving up power to the group is understandable. The good news is that Tagitude unleashes the power of the many and makes everyone an expert of their own talent. For the company or group, tagging everyone's expertise increases the speed and quality of innovation, thereby giving managers and leaders the best compass and map to navigate decisions where it matters most—in the value zone—every day. It comes down to trusting your workforce. They've already got the security code to the building, keys to the cash register, expense accounts, access to salary information and passwords for the company networks, so what's the harm in letting them identify their own talent?

In the end, power as a leader means ultimately having people on your team who are in the right positions on the right projects and using their best capabilities to deliver the objectives we have established. Leaders still have this obligation and responsibility, but now you have more information to draw from—actually, more than you've ever had before.

Proud of the Crowd

If you have been even slightly involved in any collaborative workplace initiatives, you've certainly come across the term "power of the crowd." Tagitude is about being proud of the crowd, not frightened of it. Increasingly, employees expect to be heard and we have more of an opportunity than ever before to listen. We've seen already how transparency and trust have clearly become an expectation of today's employees, and we've covered some of the questions you might have about the practicalities associated with peer-to-peer tagging. Having the right Tagitude and otherwise taking steps to make this concept viable for your company means a more robust talent pool, the identification of hidden skills and abilities in an organization, a reduction in recruitment costs, an inexpensive technology solution and much more. Tags also give managers the potential to redirect and protect their training investment, better focus their development actions and build teams with a sound strategic direction.

> "Indeed, self-organizing communities on the Web have proved time and again that they can be more effective in creating value than hierarchies—so why should it be different in the workplace? It is just a matter of shifting organizational paradigms. As self-organization becomes accepted as a viable method of production, more and more workplace processes will move from being hierarchically directed to self-organizing.
>
> **—Don Tapscott and Anthony D. Williams**
> *Wikinomics: How Mass Collaboration Changes Everything*

There's no doubt that an organization benefits by trusting employees enough to let them do things, and thereby feel as though they have a stake in the company. In his now famous book *Employees First, Customers Second: Turning Conventional Management Upside Down,* Vice Chairman and CEO of HCL Technologies Ltd. Vineet Nayar gives several examples in which this is has been key to the success of this India-based global information technology services company: "In a culture of trust in which you're pushing the envelope of transparency, we found that most people within the organization know very well what's wrong with a company, sometimes even before management does, or at least before management is willing to admit it. When you bring this information out into the open and make the challenges public, employees feel included." Nayar adds that one of the resulting payoffs to all of this is that employees oftentimes start working on problems without being asked to do so!

Many companies have been struggling with the onset of collaborative technologies and the freedom of expression it unleashes inside structures that ordinarily operate through hierarchies, policies and processes. I completely understand why many are fearful that this new world of transparency could spin out of control; our employees might say or share something mortifying, or our status in the organization could be threatened. That being said, we're left with a choice: continue to worry about what might transpire when the gatekeepers are not there to censure things, and employees are empowered more or make a fresh start with a new Tagitude—thereby using this access to social capital to gain all of the advantages of this new reality of trust and transparency.

By involving people in the process of identifying the talents of others, we all become part of the talent management process, thereby making the company stronger and more flexible when shifting resources and talent become an even more potent competitive advantage. Over the long run, Tagability enables organizations to more effectively utilize resources, as well as increase loyalty and decrease attrition. Best of all, it creates greater visibility of talent, which means less time spent searching for it.

What's in it for Me?

Hopefully by now, regardless of where you sit in the organization, you've seen the benefits of the Tagosphere and, more precisely, a good Tagitude. But like with any change initiative, the natural question may be: "What's in it for me?" Here are three things to remember:

Visibility
- of my talent
- of my team's talent
- of my colleagues' talents

Flexibility
- to use my talents where they are best suited

- to manage my teams
- to align the right people with business objectives

Possibility

- to receive ongoing feedback
- to receive more appropriate development opportunities
- to be recognized by everyone, not just my boss

We develop a symbiosis among the different roles inside an organization, be it between line managers and HR, Marketing and Communications, Tenders and Projects, Contracts and Sales, IT and Finance, and so on. Sometimes it's a smooth ecosystem and, in certain organizations, it's a constant battle between power and expertise. Again, Fraser and Dutta partly address this point: "Organizations are made up of varying interest groups and individuals, all with diverse agendas and needs. It's no wonder that it is difficult to manage, move fast and change when you combine these groups of individuals with culture, economic and resource availability factors. The difference today, however, is that trying to control these groups is less and less likely to have a successful outcome, whereas harnessing their potential group power can give us more time to focus on other controllable factors."

If you're in HR, you win all of the above, plus the bonus round. Having the right Tagitude means knowing that your job or its value isn't going to be rendered worthless by the Tagosphere. I know as well as anyone working in HR how hard it is to connect HR initiatives to business priorities, but the fact remains that HR will always be an important player in the life of a company. Adopting a good Tagitude offers an opportunity for HR to provide the organization with tools, methodologies and analytics to deploy talent optimally and drive better decision-making. In addition, it allows our various talent initiatives to be more realistic and effective, with the end game being happier employees and improved company results.

What's in it for Them?

We're going to have to ask *them* to take a salary cut.
They're never happy with the food in the cafeteria!
They won't understand the reorganization unless we explain it to *them*.
Should we let *them* bring their spouses to the company outing?
How are we going to break it to *them* that we're raising their insurance premiums?
How can we get *them* to use the new system?

"Them"? It's always difficult for me to write about "us" and "them" when referring to HR and employees because, ultimately, we are all "them" — that is, "employees." Even if we are managers or "people experts" who are paid to manage "them," coach "them," promote "them," pay "them" and so on, we are generally only one organization chart box away from *being* "them." As leaders determining policies and work rules, the decisions we make concerning "them" eventually affect us, too. If you have difficulty understanding what's in it for "them," re-read the "What's in it for me?" section directly above. And then there are shareholders and customers. What about *them*? I think you'll agree that they subsequently benefit from the value of an organization that is transparent and more responsive to the marketplace. With Tagitude and the entire Tagosphere, there is no "us" and "them," only "we" and "me."

We now know how Tagitude provides an atmosphere of support and encouragement that allows everyone the chance to give and receive the benefits of a more trusting and transparent organization. What we'll see in the next chapter is how our tagging behavior doesn't go completely unmonitored or allowed to run amok; our personal reputation, or Tagutation, guarantees this.

TAGUTATION

CHAPTER 4

/tagutation/ *noun*. how tags attributed to and given by us affect our reputation and the reputation of others.

I t's quite possible that you're at the stage of wondering how people might actually behave once given the opportunity to tag each other. Before we explore this, it's important to delve into what I call Tagutation, or your reputation as it relates to peer-to-peer tagging. To do so, we need to understand the broader context of how reputations are built (or destroyed) in the digital world today.

I invite you for a moment to consider the notion of "reputation" – what it is, why it's important and how the new social world has expanded its meaning and usage. You'll see it's much more than what people are saying about the stars on the red carpet or why the office is talking about the boss who danced on the table at the last holiday party.

Reputation Matters in More Ways Than Ever

> "It takes many good deeds to build a good reputation, and only one bad one to lose it."

> **—Benjamin Franklin**

"I don't care what others think or say about me!" How many times have you heard someone say this? Do you ever really believe it? Most of us were raised with some value system that teaches us that our actions have an impact on how people view us or behave towards us. We may disregard other people's interpretation as false or not completely accurate, but we do tend to pay attention to their perceptions. The confidence that we inspire in others (and they in us) is measured by what is called "reputation," a word that derives from the Latin root reputatio, or "evaluation." Reputation is, therefore, a social assessment or simply the opinion that one or many people have of one another; this evaluation can be given to a person, group of people or community, an organization, or a product or brand. Although we generally think of reputation in the context of good or bad, it's really neutral until we overlay our opinions. Of course, opinions are value judgments that are subjective by their very nature and are disputable, especially when those opinions stem from assumptions, rumors, prejudices and plain lies that are meant to manipulate.

Like it or not, everybody has a reputation. In previous generations, as in the era of the American Wild West during the 19th Century, your reputation was primarily built by word of mouth and no more. If two or more folks at the local saloon were talking about you, the discussion was finished and everyone went about their business, polishing their pistols or whatever. If you developed a good reputation amongst the townspeople, you could have a decent life as a ranch hand, fur trader or innkeeper. If you had a bad reputation—let's say you slept with the Sheriff's wife and were run out of town on a rail before sundown—it was possible to start afresh and rebuild your reputation by relocating to a different town where nobody knew your personal history.

Living in the Wild, Wild Web

Today's Internet frontier is a horse of a different color. With so much multi-media content being shared online through text, video and audio—then captured that way for posterity—once something is ascribed to you in the public domain, it's there for all to see and can't be left at the watering hole. Search engines can detect what you say and what is said about you, and can bring it into the homes and hands of anyone and everyone. In fact, today's social media and brand managers work full time monitoring the reputation of the organizations they work for. When you think of it in these terms, yes, you DO want to care what others think or say about you – or what you say yourself! Your words and actions not only affect the way people treat you, both on the job and in your personal life, but could potentially make or break your career.

In today's digital world—and with collaborative work environments continuing to proliferate—we need to be increasingly aware of (and concerned with) not only our reputation but our "e-reputation," or how we exist on the Web. How do you "get" an e-reputation and where is it visible? The most obvious way is that whatever you post online becomes part of it—certainly your Facebook, Twitter, Orkut, Google+, Pinterest and LinkedIn profiles—and of course, your personal or business website. Your reputation can also be impacted by the trail of comments you've posted on a variety of blogs or commercial websites. On Amazon, TripAdvisor or many e-commerce sites, for example, not only can you leave an opinion of a product, hotel or restaurant you've visited, but you can see (and we do look!) how many times this opinion was viewed as "useful" by others. If you are an online seller or buyer (such as on the ever popular eBay), you can develop an e-reputation by how accurately you describe your product, how well you communicate with bidders, and the speed and price of delivery. You never imagined how much your grandmother's mint condition Victrola could affect your reputation, did you?

Much More Than a Popularity Contest: Monitoring Your Reputation on the Web

Your online reputation is much more than the number of "likes" on your profiles, posts or pages. To a degree, "likes" are more about popularity than reputation (as we know from our school days, the most popular girl may not have the best reputation, or the least popular teacher may have a great reputation). People "liking" your posts is an acknowledgement of something you've said or done, but mostly a way to spread the word that you exist, especially to others who didn't know about you previously. It's probably safe to say that most people would like to have a healthy balance of both reputation and popularity. Online, that would equate to being referenced often (the number of times your name shows up in a search, how often your posts are shared, etc.) and what people are commenting or saying about you. You can also gauge your online reputation through other things that are quantitative, if not qualitative. They include: the number of contacts and recommendations you have on Xing; the number of comments you chalk up on your blog posts; how many Twitter followers you have; or how much online influence is demonstrated by your Klout score.

There are other ways to learn about your reputation on the Web. With Google and Bing, you can type your name into a search engine to see how many times you are referenced in the virtual world. Sites such as Yatedo, 123people and PeopleFinders show you in real time where your name or photo might be floating around. And if you think that comment you made about calling in sick so you could nurse your hangover won't be visible because you've carefully chosen your privacy settings, you may find the following quite sobering.

Callum Haywood from the UK created what he calls "a social network privacy experiment" in 2012, when he was 18 years old. The former site WeKnowWhatYou'reDoing.com cleverly aggregated public status updates from social networking platforms like Facebook and Foursquare. The experiment classified status updates under headings such as:

- Who wants to be fired?
- Who has a hangover?
- Who takes drugs?
- Who has a new phone number?

You might be thinking, I don't partake in (or at least divulge) any of this, so I have nothing to worry about. But now imagine replacing or adding to those categories with comments related to religion, politics, sex or any other number of things you might not want to share with the entire world. Or let's say you discover a photo you were tagged in appears on your friend's newsfeed without your knowledge, along with an entire discussion about you. I think you get the picture. Even though steps are being taken in the cyber world to protect people's privacy and sites like Haywood's have ceased to exist, it's still important to remember that what you have "out there" can be seen.

All of these sites are successful, or at least intriguing, because of a little voice inside our head that asks, "What can people see about me?" or "What can I find out about someone?" If this wasn't the case, there wouldn't be so much debate about data privacy, the security of your personal information and how to "leave an application" without leaving a trace. You can already engage services from companies like Reputation.com and BrandYourself.

com who will help you control what people find when they search for you on the Web. And if you're still not sleeping at night, companies like SwissLife and Axa now tout insurance that protects against not only identity theft and other types of fraud but also damage to your e-reputation. With such a policy, private information or undesirable data that is published about you on the Web can be erased. (In fact, you could hire an online reputation management agency like The Reputation Squad to do it for you.) And if you think it's difficult to manage your reputation today, don't forget that it will continue after you go to that Big Chat Room in the sky. But fear not, there are even Internet services that will help your heirs manage your e-presence in the digital afterlife.

With or Without You: Building, Monitoring and Defending Your Reputation

Taking all of this into consideration, it should be obvious that your online reputation is being formulated whether you're aware of it or not. And for those of you who are not especially active on social media, not being there doesn't necessarily help either. "Ignoring the issue of your online reputation doesn't mean that your reputation doesn't exist," explains my colleague Olivier Zara, an expert in e-reputation. "Wouldn't you rather have some control over it? It happens with or without you, so it makes digital common sense to manage this risk by being proactive instead of reacting." You may not be able to completely control your e-reputation, but you can effectively manage it—not by trying to block what people say or think about you, but by being aggressive in monitoring and building your reputation and if need be, defending it.

Being proactive about your reputation is probably the best way to protect it. Even if you do not produce content, your "media space" is occupied by others (including your competitors and peers), by what people say about you, blog about you or your products, or even by people who bear the same name as you (and can be confused for being you). It is also possible to have a good reputation in the physical world and an unfavorable one in the digital world, and for your online reputation to destroy the professional and personal reputation that you've been diligent at keeping pristine.

Managing your reputation on the Internet is just like in real life, except with a technical twist: By monitoring when and where your name is mentioned online, you'll know when someone is saying something about you and can act quickly. For example, if someone is blogging about you, using your music or publishing your copyrighted work without permission, you will have the ability to respond appropriately, if needed. I am not suggesting that it's an easy, clear-cut job; you may not be able to prevent someone from right-clicking and copying your photos.

> **Build your professional reputation.** You can do this in various ways. Start a blog, publish a news article or academic research, give recommendations and customer testimonials, offer a case study on your expertise, and post appropriate photos and videos.

> **Monitor your reputation.** Use sites or applications such as Google Alerts, Naymz, People123 and MyPermissions to know what others are saying about you or posting as you.

> **Defend your reputation.** When necessary, respond to attacks on your name or brand, and take steps to hide or erase traces of things that negatively affect your reputation. This includes image rights, the right to privacy, defamation, legal proceedings and mutual agreements. Keep in mind

the distinction between negative opinions and freedom of speech, and be aware of the confusion between defamation and negative opinion.[5]

None of this is meant to scare you but rather make to you aware. "Learning to monitor and, if necessary, defend your digital reputation will soon become as important as learning to read and write," Zara said. Effectively monitoring your online reputation has its advantages. You have the means to know everything that is being said about you. In real life, you may have a bad reputation because others are talking about you behind your back; when someone attacks your reputation on the Internet, it's public. But we can't disengage from the online conversation. If we do, it's a bit like talking to ourselves in the street!

Your Reputation Inside the Company

You may have already made the leap as to how some of the issues surrounding your reputation outside of your company can be easily compared to how you manage your reputation inside an organization. We'll get to that in a minute. But first, as you'll see in the following story, your online presence (and more importantly, how you manage it) can have a big effect on your reputation and career when the social and professional aspects begin to overlap.

I'm in the Apple Retail Store in Paris after several unsuccessful attempts to install the new OS on my iPhone. I walk in knowing that it's one of the few places where I can really count on someone to help me solve a technical problem. Philippe is the lucky Apple specialist who gets to resolve my concern. While Philippe reloads my address book, he makes a comment.

---

[5]   *A Successful Career With Personal Branding -Olivier Zara, 2009*

"Monsieur, you've got a lot of contacts—more than 1,300. You should think about deleting some of them."

I glare at him, surprised. "Why? How many do you have?"

"I've got 137," he says proudly.

I chuckle to myself and make a joke about how my being decades older than him must be the reason why I'd amassed so many. Then I launch into my usual helpful HR coaching mode – I can act like the HR police at times —and ask Philippe if he has a LinkedIn profile.

"Nah... I've heard that I should," he said. "But then your bosses can see you there, and they watch what you do or think you're looking for a job."

Now I'm really surprised. Here's Philippe, a young IT geek (meant with the fondest admiration) who works for one of the most tech-savvy companies in the world, and even he doesn't seem to appreciate the importance of having a professional network, let alone having an interest in putting his profile on one of the planet's largest social business networking sites. How can this be? To me, it's unfathomable! Something must be done! I take it on as my moral imperative to set Philippe straight on this matter, explaining that no doubt every one of his bosses is probably already on LinkedIn, and if one day he ever wants to stop dealing with dummies like me who can't figure out their own smartphones, he should be developing his business network now.

"Yeah, I hear Google is opening offices in Paris," Philippe says, now pondering my unsolicited advice.

"That's right, and I happen to know that they have at least six job ads listed on LinkedIn right now."

"Really?" Philippe asks. "Hmm... maybe I should be on LinkedIn. But won't my boss be able to see that I'm looking for a new job?" he asks.

Over the next few minutes, I explain that his boss can only view certain things and that it's he who controls what people can and cannot see. I explain that, conversely, he can see what the boss is doing there, so both parties have a mutual interest in managing their level of visibility within the system.

I ask Philippe if he uses Facebook.

"Bien sûr! But only with my personal friends and a few close co-workers —never my boss!"

"And why's that?" I ask provokingly.

"If he could see how I spend my weekends with my friends, I'm not sure he'd appreciate it," he says with a wink.

"So you see," I tell him, "You're already managing the way you're viewed and by whom. It's the same with your professional online network."

We talk a bit more about the pros and cons of a business social networking site, but his fear about protecting his reputation at his current job is now less of a hurdle.

I say "merci" and leave him with these thoughts. He agrees to join LinkedIn and I agree to look again at those 1,300 contacts in my address book.

Philippe's story illustrates the mindset that many people have regarding the division between their personal and professional Web presence. This dilemma often arises due to the different contexts and decision-making points that are integral to each platform. Most networking and collaborative tools generally offer the same options (comment, share, upload a photo, post a link, tag, etc.) and we as users (as well as the community at large) decide how to behave on these platforms. It determines our activity and, consequently, our reputation. By and large, we have become pretty adept at knowing what to post and where, even if sometimes we have to learn by trial and error.

Your Employee Reputation is Your Personal Brand

In much the same way that your reputation on the Web comes together over time with the content you contribute, your reputation inside a company is built through your contributions on the job and how others perceive you. Social networks, forums, profiles and blogs have made it easier to build a brand—personal and professional—like in the real world, just showing up (or having an e-presence) isn't enough. In social media, you must be a resource, not a spammer. The same holds true within a company; whether it's in the virtual world or at your workplace, your contributions—what can be called "content"—have to provide a level of value in terms of advancing a goal or an objective. How you "distribute" this content (lead, educate, inform or even entertain) has to be consistently fresh and reflect your career and business objectives. Today we must concern ourselves with our e-presence and e-reputation, yet we have been managing our employee brand long before everything began with an "e."

How we perform our jobs, communicate with colleagues, conduct ourselves in meetings, share knowledge or expertise, treat our customers and suppliers, and even the respect we give or have bestowed upon us all helps to shape the perceptions and reputation that we develop over the course of our careers. This comes naturally to most of us; otherwise, we wouldn't survive a day at work.

EmployEE Branding

You've probably heard the term "employer branding," which is essentially the way a company positions itself as an employer of choice in the employment marketplace. And you might have heard about "personal branding," or the way we present or package ourselves to the world (our name, style, knowledge, words and deeds). However, we miss something quite obvious if we don't reflect on the concept of how our acts and personality are conveyed daily in the workplace, or what I call "employEE branding."

EmployEE branding is interesting to look at in the context of Tagutation because it combines our reputation on and off the Web with what we already know about the effects of our behavior, presentation, status and positioning in a company. In this sense, it helps to create our "professional" brand. If what we say and do (and what others say about us) is important outside of the office, then the same impressions that people have of us at work—when there's a correlation to promotions, salaries, training and development opportunities and so forth—is probably even more critical. Why else would we take greater care with what we say and do and how we say and do it in our job, than when we post a silly joke or video on the Web? Some will argue that personal branding is the same whether it's inside or outside of a formal hierarchical structure such as a company or enterprise, and they wouldn't be incorrect. However, we must agree that except for very few of us, we manage our brand differently as an employee (even if unconsciously) than we do with, say, a university buddy whom we reconnect with at a school reunion 20 years later.

Benefits, training, career opportunities and ethics are just some ways in which companies build their employer brand. It can also be a reflection of the working environment that the company creates and how happy its employees are. (Look at sites such as Glassdoor.com and Meilleurs-Entreprise.com to see where your company rates.) If we're happy as employees, we become walking-talking advertisements for the company.

EmployEE branding, on the other hand, is not just about how good of an ambassador you are for the company brand but how well you represent yourself amongst your colleagues and peers, project team members, and your current or future boss. In the end, your people should be ambassadors for your brand, but it's not exclusively about the company. What I'm talking about is having the employee build his personal brand for the benefit of the employee himself, which ultimately helps the company.

All of this talk about our reputation and brand is pertinent in the Tagosphere to illustrate clearly that they are evolving minute by minute. Even if we're not as conscious of our reputation as we could be, it is governing our behavior and provides the foundation of our Tagutation.

Managing Your Tagutation

Practically since the dawn of civilization, there has been a "give and take" amongst the individuals in any given clan, community or society. If someone does something for you, you're more likely to do something for that person in return. If a neighbor agrees to stop by your apartment and water your plants while you're on a business trip, you may feel inclined to bring a gift back from that trip as a "thank you" or return the favor when that neighbor needs something. If not, you may develop the reputation as a "taker" and your neighbor may be less likely to help you out next time. Similarly, if you get tagged by a colleague, you're more prone to return the action. I call this the "tag back" principle; if someone tags me, I feel inclined to respond in kind. I may even be secretly hoping that they will tag me back. If others are tagged and I'm not, I might become hurt or even concerned that nobody is tagging me and will find a way to be tagged.

You may have noticed the same feelings when asking or being asked to write a recommendation for someone on LinkedIn. I'll talk more about that in a minute because the impact of tags and recommendations are quite different, but the give-and-take concept still exists. "When people recommend me on LinkedIn, it feels good and encourages me to recommend them back, even though they haven't asked," says Rhonda Bernard, Learning and Talent Management Director, EMEA for Estée Lauder Companies Europe. "Of course, I'm not completely naïve. Recommendations are designed to work this way, but there's still something about reading positive statements from my network that makes me want to do the same for them."

The same is true with LinkedIn's endorsement function. So many people I speak with say that they get endorsed by people they either don't know or who don't know enough about them to endorse them yet, deep down, they appreciate the attention. What you may not realize, however, is that this collection of skills is a database of talent for other services provided by the company, such as recruitment, sales, etc.

So if giving and taking has a mutual effect, what can we expect behavior to be like when tagging our colleagues? Generally speaking, people will carefully manage their Tagutation because their employEE brand depends on it. If our reputation outside of work is important to us, then it's logical that our employEE brand will be just as important because our next promotion, relocation assignment or salary increase can hinge on how people perceive us. Building, monitoring and defending our Tagutation is why people will be careful about what they say about themselves and others within the Tagosphere.

Your Tagutation, when combined with Tagitude, is transparent; everyone can see who is tagging whom. When your employEE brand is at stake, tagging somebody a "jerk," "stupid," "political" or "obnoxious" impacts us as much as the person we tagged. We all have an opinion of the person we know who always shoots off a nasty email before thinking about it. But when the entire organization is on copy, we are helpless to do anything about it. Fortunately, within the Tagosphere, individuals have more control over contributions because they hold veto power, and Tagutation discourages this from the start.

In a recent presentation I was giving on the subject, an attendee shouted out the question, "What if a group of employees get together and decide to give each other a bunch of tags to make themselves look good?" My response was that with Tagutation, employees are unlikely to risk not only giving but accumulating "false" tags, or "Tag Spam." False tags can't be backed up with actions, and as we saw in Tagability, it still takes a large number of the same tag to become meaningful to the total picture. Will there be somebody in the company who runs a subversive campaign to promote themselves? Possibly (frankly, I've seen everything), but their tags are still just one piece of the puzzle that completes the picture of their employee brand. I'm quite confident that the mutual tagging coup (coup d'éTag?) is a low-risk scenario.

Tagutation Versus Recommendations

In decades past, you could almost be guaranteed a job if you had the right "hard" skills, such as welding, plumbing and driving. As automation and new technologies required a change in workforce dynamics and the job market became more competitive, companies started looking for "soft" skills such as speaking, listening, communication, organization and leadership. In today's job market, employees must consider three things: their hard skills, their soft skills and their online influence. As crazy as this might have sounded in pre-historic times—that is, 20 years ago (especially since very few people had heard about social media) – it is highly possible today that a Marketing professional might be hired into a job position based on the number of Twitter followers he has or if Oprah is retweeting him. Individuals who have the largest and most influential networks bring more to a company than simply their professional skills; they also now bring an audience of potential customers.

Now you may not have Oprah following you, but as you're reading this chapter, you may be making comparisons to sites where you request or leave a recommendation or other type of endorsement. As we just read about Rhonda Bernard's experience of receiving recommendations, it's clear that these aren't going away anytime soon. But are they effective?

First, let's remind ourselves that recommendations are nothing new. When we ask a friend to recommend a doctor, mechanic, school system or recipe, we simply pick up the phone (or meet them in person) and receive all the benefits of their advice. Recruiters and employers still evaluate a candidate's professional reputation from a person's spoken or written references. It might not last much longer, but today, reference checking goes a little bit like this: After a job interview—which recruiters use to validate their feelings vis-à-vis candidates and probe deeper into other aspects of a prospect's career and personality—though company might make a few phone calls to a candidate's previous employer to check out the person's reputation. Today in the U.S. and other countries, asking for references from previous employers is essentially ineffective due to legal constraints; the process is reduced to calling the three people given by the candidate as references and obtaining verification that the employee did work for them, their dates of employment and their last salary. It just goes to show how one's e-reputation has become even more important, and as such, the campaign to get recommendations added to your profile is a preoccupation by some.

When you send an email asking for recommendations, it's a campaign that in and of itself contributes to your reputation. Yet a campaign of soliciting recommendations is different from people spontaneously writing recommendations and the impact is different. Similarly, we know that there are many professionals who are excessive with their use of social networks. Constant requests to "write a recommendation" or "put me in touch with somebody else" can be viewed unfavorably as a purely commercial, self-promoting exercise. I once knew a man who parted ways with his company, and the first thing he did during his job search was launch an email blast to every one of his contacts asking for online recommendations. I warned him of the consequences but his reaction was somewhat bitter. "I'm going to see who writes them to know who I can trust." Well, because it's a small world, I started hearing from mutual contacts that they had received requests that they didn't feel qualified or even willing to fulfill. Just by conducting this recommendation campaign, he developed an unfavorable reputation amongst a number of his contacts.

So how useful are recommendations? "If they are in someone's profile, I basically use it to just look up what the person has done," says Kristen Smit, Managing Director and Partner at Executive Search firm Boyden Paris. "I'm also usually kind of curious to see who and where those recommendations come from, because sometimes they are not directly related to what the person actually does. If I really need to know details, I'll call the person directly." It should also be noted that recruiters are being paid to not only search for candidates, but to screen for the best ones. They don't necessarily like recommendations because they are also trying to find what's wrong with a person. Since a recommendation is always positive, the greatest value it brings search consultants is the ability to see who wrote it and from what company or organization.

Now the bad news... Online recommendations, although often flattering, are probably not producing the results we intend for them. What I can say is that writing recommendations engages our own reputation. We only write what we'd be comfortable with others seeing. If I say somebody's a good program manager that I'd be pleased to work with again, it means that I engage my personal reputation; however, with tags, it's now my employee reputation that is at risk, so I must be doubly sure of what I write.

The other shortcoming of recommendations is that people don't know how to write them very effectively—and need I add, they are lengthy and time-consuming to compose, unless you use one of the computer-generated recommendations websites. It's not like an annual performance review where we say: "Here are your good points and bad points and places to improve." It's a recommendation, and a recommendation is always positive. Getting people to write recommendations is another story. They can sound flowery and embellished, and leave out important factors that describe successful actions in a professional context with related behavior and results. We know it has to be positive but people write them according to their own inspiration or motivation, and may even use words they have seen in other recommendations that they've read. But with writing, things become complicated. It's difficult to search for, it takes too long to read and the same sentence can be interpreted in various ways; for example: "he was a special member of my team," or "working with him was interesting."

Tags, as we've seen, are positive like a recommendation, but also short, specific and searchable. Written recommendations are nearly impossible to use to search for talent, and even resume mining systems, besides being a snapshot of experience, can be manipulated if you know how to include key words. The recent onslaught of requests for endorsements is a perfect example. Key words magically appear below someone's photo derived from their profile. You are asked to recommend or endorse this particular skill. They are their words, not yours, and we tend to "go EWOT" (Endorse Without Thinking). There's no risk to this because your employee reputation won't be affected. With Tagutation, you tag the talent when you see it, with your own words, and because your reputation is at stake, it's authentic. What's more, tags are easier to write than sentences so more data can be collected in less space. The visual representation of one's reputation can thus be checked in a matter of seconds, and the sender doesn't waste time writing them because all he has to do is tag a few words or phrases.

In 2006, Olivier Zara developed what was probably the first use of tagging for describing one's reputation in the public domain. His CV 2.0 software is a perfect example of the use of tagging to consolidate one's professional references through recommendations (where one's tag cloud can serve as a "reputational" tag cloud, not just "informational"). The software is pretty powerful and super easy to use. With one click you have a visual representation of someone's reputation. Zara's idea was to describe one's reputation with tags so that a person's reputation could be easily seen whether they have three personal references or 300 tags. So if tagging can serve as recommendations by our colleagues in the company without raising our boss' concern that we're job hunting, we get the best of both worlds.

Tagutation as a Form of Employee Referral

Employee referral programs have been around now for quite some time, and companies have seen the benefit of their employees identifying and pre-screening potential colleagues, while simultaneously serving as ambassadors of the employer brand. Depending on the skill set being sought, companies have been known to pay anywhere from $250 to $2,500 to $10,000 on bonuses to an employee who refers a candidate that is hired. Although there are several benefits, the basic underlying premise of these programs can be broken down as follows:

- Employees have a broader network of profiles sought by the company.
- A bonus to an employee is less expensive than typical recruitment expenses.
- Employees will recommend high-quality candidates who will not adversely affect their employee brand or personal reputation.

If we compare the Tagosphere to employee referral programs, we can see several similarities. Just as employees know qualified people outside of the company, their network is equally as broad inside by virtue of their job roles and activities. They come across a wide range of "candidate" profiles every day and know who's good at what. The Digital Single Processing Engineer knows the best Digital Single Processing Engineer, and who better to identify the best ICU nurse than an ICU nurse? "Although employee referrals work extremely well for external hires, most corporations have no internal process where employees can make referrals for open jobs," says John Sullivan, a management professor at San Francisco State University. Tagging can fill the void. Like employee referrals, Tagutation reinforces the premise that employees will be more vested in the quality of talent they identify. They will identify the best talent in the least amount of time, which ultimately will speed up the integration of this talent in the future. And taken one step further, it doesn't get any cheaper than using peer recommendations through tags to "refer" employees internally.

Upcycle Your Brand

Whether you're happy with your brand and simply want to reinforce it, or feel that it needs a facelift and want to completely reinvent it, Tagutation offers some unique opportunities. Tagutation reinforces what you already do as a way to promote your employee brand but in bite-size, yet powerful pieces of information. Over time, your Tagutation becomes more visible, but not in a brash, show-off kind of way.

Not everybody is comfortable with the idea of promoting oneself or being too visible. This can be a result of our job function, education or ingrained references such as personal upbringing, religious beliefs or culture. No doubt, "reputation" means different things to different people. In some cultures, it's acceptable or even expected that you stand out; in others, it isn't. In some cultures, people like to know who you are and attribute your reputation by who you know; in others, it's more about what you do. Celebrities are known to reinvent themselves according to their audience or the times, but even Madonna knows it takes longer than one costume change to create a new image. That being said, inside the Tagosphere, we have a unique opportunity to do just that.

Those of you who feel like you've been pigeonholed have an opportunity to re-brand yourselves. Not only will the tags your peers and colleagues attribute to you help bring to the foreground otherwise unseen talents, you can also zoom in on the talents you want to be known for. Now, the employee known as a superb technical writer by his boss has the opportunity to be noticed by the Marketing and Communications Department. A new Tagutation can serve as an aperture that opens up career possibilities that could benefit the employee and the company. Great companies already recognize these cross-functional opportunities. Unfortunately, too many companies still put people into a box based on their work history or organization's competency model. Tagutation gives employees a new tool to open the box; inside, companies will find an abundance of hidden potential.

Tagutation is Blind

One of the less apparent benefits of the Tagosphere is that Tagutation can help make visible certain individuals in an organization who may otherwise go unnoticed or neglected because of attitudes, assumptions, misconceptions or prejudices. People with physical or cognitive disabilities have been dealing with these inequities in the workplace for years, but technology has been opening doors for many of them that were previously inaccessible. Internet job postings and virtual career fairs (where an entire interview can be conducted by chat or video) have expanded the ways that anyone can look for new employment. Just as online career fairs give people with disabilities a fair chance to be seen and recognized first for their talents, tagging is similar. Peers may know your physical limitations or other discriminating factors, the person responsible for finding talent in the organization may not.

The Administrative Assistant who is disabled may have never been considered for a project or transfer because the organization just assumed she wouldn't be up for the task. Her colleagues may be perfectly aware and supportive of her strengths and limitations, but her boss may only see her physical handicap. However, her job takes her all over the world by telephone and she touches internal clients each day with her efficiency, excellent customer service and penchant for numbers. Through tagging, her talents can be visible to the entire organization first, and her disability last.

The talent manager seeking someone who is good with numbers will see her talents on a par with others who have the same skill.

The same can hold true for other diversity issues like gender, race, age and sexual orientation—by giving employees the opportunity to develop a Tagutation around their talents, maybe even providing the first opportunity to demonstrate and communicate their talents more widely. Your tags, like an online career fair, can get your foot in the door based on what you know and what you can do, not how you are.

One practical example of the use of tagging as it relates to gender was when it was integrated into an innovative program at Carnegie Mellon University. The Negotiation Academy for Women brought together 24 female executives with the objective of teaching them how to become strong negotiators. The Program Director, MJ Tocci, saw a perfect application for tagging between participants, their networks and coaches. "It is well known that women are the best negotiators for others," said Tocci. "They negotiate household budgets, conflicting schedules and things like their children's school and extracurricular activities. Behind the scenes, they can even be powerhouse negotiators for their spouses' compensation package or next big job assignment," Tocci said. "But when it comes to the workplace, they tend to be very weak in negotiating their own salary and promotion opportunities. If I could introduce a way for them to learn what talents others see in them, I can show them how to use these talents to negotiate a whole lot better in every aspect of their lives."

YUMP Academy is (another) good example of eluding the typical path to success by harnessing the value of peer-to-peer tagging. This start-up incubator is aimed at giving disadvantaged groups of people from the Paris suburbs the opportunity to create a company, something many of them in the normal "system" would never have the opportunity to do otherwise. Not only did they receive coaching by business professionals, they were given the opportunity to tag each other during their 6-month program with skills and behaviors their co-participants noticed in each of them. With 43% of the individuals not even having a high school diploma, this was a rare opportunity to not only receive feedback, but to learn what it was like to give feedback. Something that most privileged leaders even have trouble with!

As we've seen, our reputation and brands all project a little more about who we are and what we're about. Tagutation certainly helps us become visible—with an added value of giving everyone a fair shot at showing their talents and possibly being identified for that next great job.

TAGOGNITION

CHAPTER 5

/tagognition/ *noun.* the emotional result achieved from the giving or receiving of tags by peers, leading to a sense of recognition and self-actualization.

Movie stars crave it. Politicians lie for it. Celebrity chefs hunger for it. Boy Scouts merit it. Dogs roll over for it. Business schools teach it. Maslow says we need it. Recognition. Anybody who's ever taken a basic psychology course, attended a leadership program or is the parent of a child (or in a relationship with someone who acts like a child), knows all too well Abraham Maslow's hierarchy of needs. We all seek to be accepted, respected and valued as individuals. And being that we spend most of our waking hours at work (unless you sleep on the job), it only makes sense that this innate need for social recognition, status and even prestige shows up on the job. None of this is news, really. In your earliest Management 101 class, last week's leadership webinar, or somewhere in between, you've no doubt run across Maslow and Co. or other research that confirms our fundamental need for esteem. Every manager knows that giving recognition is a good thing. Every company tries to do it. Yet we struggle to translate this warm-and-fuzzy concept into concrete business results. When budgets get tight, the first things to go are training, travel and a whole assortment of feel-good perks. Tagognition brings people and business results together. Before we can appreciate the benefits of Tagognition, it's important to remind ourselves of the powerful effects of recognition. A 2012 study from Bersin & Associates, a leading provider of research-based membership programs in human resources (HR), talent and learning, showed that companies that excel at employee recognition are 12 times more likely on average to generate strong business results than their peers.[6] "Used correctly, employee recognition is an important talent management tool that can help guide employee performance, maintain increased employee engagement, reduce employee turnover, and ultimately drive business performance," the research concluded.

According to a 2016 Gallup survey, "only one in three workers in the U.S. strongly agree that they received recognition or praise for doing good work in the past seven days. At any given company, it's not uncommon for employees to feel that their best efforts are routinely ignored. Further, employees who do not feel adequately recognized are twice as likely to say they'll quit in the next year."[7]

So what's the trickle-down effect? Well, even if you have the best people you could possibly dream of having on your team, if they don't feel openly and honestly communicated with, they aren't going to stick around. Just ask the headhunters. This doesn't mean that we have to only tell our employees

---

[6]   *"New Bersin & Associates Research." Bersin by Deloitte. Deloitte. Viewed March 1, 2017.* http://www.bersin.com/News/Content.aspx?id=16023

[7]   *"Business Journal June 28, 2016." Gallup.com. Annamarie Mann and Nate Dvorak. Viewed March 1, 2017.* http://www.gallup.com/businessjournal/193238/employee-recognition-low-cost-high-impact.aspx

wonderful things; in fact, they don't want that, either. They just want the truth. If I know what I'm good at and not good at, and I can have an honest discussion about it, then I bet I'll do the best I can with what I've got. And it works both ways. With Tagognition, employees can now give feedback to the boss in a way that isn't uncomfortable or pandering.

With research increasingly corroborating that employee recognition is good for business, why don't top managers make it more of a priority? Well, they may be good at finance, sales or operations but giving recognition may not come naturally for some. They may see the need for recognition as selfish, unnecessary or something they've lived without (so why can't everyone else?). For others, it may not be obvious how one links to the other. To them, giving bonuses, salary increases and performance feedback is the only cause and effect they're looking for in order to keep their employees satisfied until the following year. And maybe the most challenging is that the world of recognition may be evolving faster than everyone realizes. The explosion of social media has drawn out the power of recognition in ways that are unprecedented – most notably, that recognition is immediate, instant and in real-time. Today, it's possible for an introvert from a small town anywhere in the world to get second-by-second feedback on his status updates from his thousands of "friends" via his mobile device. No matter the social media platform, the same behavior holds true no matter where we are in the world; we "like" and "share" things that people post, and we appreciate it when the "like" or "share" is reciprocated. We also look for people to comment on our activities, giving us a sense of gratification, worth and appreciation. On Twitter or Weibo, we measure our success by the number of followers we amass. On LinkedIn, European equivalent Xing and China's Sina Weibo, we check to see how many people have viewed our profile or jumped in on discussions we've started. On Pinterest, others "repin" items from our boards and acknowledge the things we're interested in. Bloggers get lots of feedback on their posts—everything from people commenting on them to reposting them in the blogosphere (a sure validation that what they are writing about has sharable value). All of these are new forms of recognition. So why is it that in companies, we neglect to tell others that we like them or we like something about them? And if we do, we seem to always go to the same bag of tricks and pull out training, money or stock options as a way to send the message—goodies that are not immediate.

The receiving of instant feedback is certainly a growing expectation, since we experience it every day outside of the office, although I'd venture to guess that people are getting their social fix from their smartphones behind their desks or in the seclusion of the restroom. So with this incurable addiction for recognition, the question quickly becomes how to apply it within a company, while also realizing a business benefit. Sharing the latest cat video probably isn't going to go down too well with the Executive Committee.

Vitamin R

Tagognition is an opportunity to apply immediate social recognition for the mutual benefit of employees and the company. Not only are skills uncovered that render the organization more agile and competitive, it also gives employees positive feedback from their peers without delay. As an added bonus, it can be a lot of fun.

Tagognition is quite straightforward and simple to understand. When you tag yourself, you identify what talents you have or where you think your strengths lie. In doing so, think of it as giving yourself a dose of positive reinforcement vitamins—let's call it "Vitamin R." When you tag others, you supplement their daily requirement of feel-good feedback. When others reciprocate, you receive the same. Even if you don't agree with their tags, the fact that they noticed something talented about you gives you yet another dose of recognition. Multiply this peer-to-peer recognition by the number of employees and you create a culture that makes the entire company healthy.

I'm certainly not naïve about human behavior. I realize that not everyone dispenses compliments easily, and that another's success can be viewed by some as hazardous to their own career. Granted, the world may not be altruistic by nature, but the student who is encouraged by her teacher to learn tries harder than the one who is embarrassed in front of the class. But I also know that we don't always feel comfortable giving feedback and it has different interpretations around the world. To top it all off, HR pros will agree that the whole predicament with Human Resources is that humans are involved. Oftentimes, we don't know what motivational solutions will work when dealing with individuals or teams. A company golf tournament is just what the doctor ordered for the boss, but maybe not for everybody. That team-building outing in the woods where you have to swing on ropes and support each other is exciting to some, but dreaded by others. And have you ever heard them say: "Just give me the money instead of spending it on the company picnic"? I have! "Recognition is not a gadget. It is not a tool kit. If it was, it would be easy for everybody and recognition would work everywhere," says Christophe Laval, author of A Plea for Recognition in the Workplace and founder of Vision, Performance and Human Recognition (VPHR), the first employee recognition company in France. "What I've learned from being a CEO for several companies is that it's very easy to improve business performance by cutting overhead, marketing and other expenses with short- to medium-term results. If we would only take two minutes to think about it, we would factor in the hidden costs related to absenteeism, disengagement, turnover and customer loyalty. Research shows that mutual recognition has a positive effect on all of these things." Tagognition won't solve the motivation and recognition problem on its own, and your company undoubtedly has its own operational and performance priorities; however, you should be able to see the potential ROI (Return on Investment) associated with tying recognition to your business goals. But the ROM (Return on Me) can be just as valuable as the bottom line.

In addition to exposing hidden competencies to the entire organization, Tagognition is part of the "giving back" that employees expect from us. I'd like you to see how simply tagging others can have a huge impact on relationships at work, while providing managers and HR with more data to manage the talents they have on their teams. Through Tagognition, we can be proactive in ensuring employee satisfaction in the first place.

One innovative way I've seen peer tagging used was by an e-Learning company in Montreal. They ran what they call Bootcamp, a conference of 300+ Human Resource, L&D and eLearning professionals from all over Canada. Instead of asking participants to fill in evaluation sheets following each speaker, they were asked to tag the speakers through a form in their program booklet. Just tags... no long sentences. They tagged Roles, Skills and Behaviors for each speaker and on the last day of the conference, these were fed back to the entire conference, by speaker, in a tag cloud. "You should have seen the room," recalls CEO Hugues Foltz. "Some speakers were so surprised that so many tags could be generated in such a short time. One commented that he never knew people found his presentation humorous and funny—thinking it was natural—while another asked if he could show his tag cloud to his wife!"

Spreading the Love

By now I'm sure you know that gone are the days when employees are loyal to institutions and motivated strictly by financial rewards and security, although many managers are still cut from this cloth (and may find it difficult to deal with the generation of employees that are more impatient, confident, eco-conscious and technologically savvy.) Perhaps in the past, employees believed that "hard work brings its own rewards" or "It's all a well thought-out plan and I just have to work hard to get what I want." That attitude is so yesterday. Kevin McKee of UK-based Cole-McKee Partnership, a consultancy specializing in helping companies maneuver through business transformation, puts it like this: "People make a mistake in thinking that their organization, their company, is like their parents. They're not. They could care less. Get over it. As long as people continue to think of them like that, they will be eternally disappointed. People still want to be a part of something. They would still love to feel that the organization cares about them even when by and large they don't. It's a basic human drive to want to belong and feel that someone cares and will look after you. But it's an illusion really. Organizations, unfortunately, encourage the illusion, which I think is a rather cynical thing. When employees are recognized by their peers, it can fill the gap left by managers who don't 'spread the love' often enough, and also to those same managers who feel they are not getting recognition, either." With Tagognition, the mindset within the organization quickly shifts from "everybody's complaining that nobody gives me recognition" to "everybody is getting recognized for what they are doing and contributing."

INFORMAL FEEDBACK:

```
Builds more engagement capital when received from
peers, rather than the manager.

Delivered through the team has a 60% greater impact
on engagement capital than informal feedback from
a direct manager.

Moreover, teams are slightly more effective at
providing informal feedback than managers.[8]
```

---

[8]   *Building Engagement Capital. Creating and Leveraging Sustainable Employee Engagement. , 2011 The Corporate Executive Board*

We have to admit that we sometimes treat internal people worse when we're recruiting someone from the outside. That may come as some sort of shock, but I've seen it time and time again. We pull out all the stops to communicate the company's vision and strategy to a candidate. We wine and dine and entice them with our sophisticated career path models, training programs and promises of a world with no limits or boundaries to what they can achieve if they join us. Then they come on board and the emphasis shifts to making sure they are productive as soon as possible. In the past, employees may have felt stuck at the company they're with, but today they see opportunity all around them. If we don't recognize their talent within our company, someone else will, because employees no longer have limited options on how or where to find a job. They've got millions of possibilities at their fingertips, and they're all just a few clicks away. Connections are being made faster than ever.

Gauging the Weather: Tagognition and Engagement

We try everything to help gauge the state of employees' commitment and overall mindset towards the organization, including engagement surveys, pulse surveys and employee opinion checkpoints. Just for fun, here are a few standard engagement survey questions that I'm sure you've come across either as an employee or as an implementer. If you had to rate them, what kind of score would you give? If your employees had to answer, what would they say?

Rate from 1 to 5 (1 = low, 5 = high)

	1	2	3	4	5
I am given sufficient feedback about my performance.					
I have adequate opportunities for professional growth in this organization.					
My manager is interested in my professional development and advancement.					
My supervisor gives me praise and recognition when I do a good job.					
I feel that I am trusted.					
There is a strong feeling of teamwork and cooperation in this organization.					
My manager treats all his/her employees fairly.					
I am encouraged in my efforts.					
The organization's policies for promotion and advancement are always fair.					
Favoritism is not an issue in raises or promotions.					
I feel that my skills and talents are well used.					

Besides the time it takes to design the survey, along with the logistics and methodology to deploy it, these so-called "climate surveys" only measure the state of mind of employees during a *fixed* period in time. But just like the weather, things change fast: people; positions; the economy; the market; and the business itself.

Conversely, let's take the case of the websites people use to search for products and services online. Consumers are continually rating and leaving feedback on these sites, and the companies are observing, analyzing and using what people say so they can change quickly to maintain or secure customers for the future. Isn't that what we want to do in the enterprise world: receive ongoing feedback and secure employees for the long term? Whether or not your organization conducts such surveys is really not the point here. Your employees ask themselves these questions every morning before deciding to get up and go back to the grind. They ask themselves these questions and more when they're out with their friends and comparing work stories. They ask themselves these questions every time a headhunter calls. What if you could increase these scores and give employees a sense of recognition for their talents and visibility on a daily basis? "The degree of respect and value [employees] feel for the contributions they make at work will significantly determine how engaged they are to give the discretionary effort for a company, their willingness to stay with the organization, or even recommend their company to family and friends as a good place to work," writes Roy Saundersen, founder and president of the Real Recognition Management Institute, in his book *GIVING the Real Recognition Way*.[9] "Employee recognition strongly impacts scores on employee satisfaction, which in turn affects performance and motivation." And all CEOs and managers worth their weight in gold know that recognition has a profound impact on productivity, morale and retention, even if it's not always evident in their daily actions.

---

[9]   *Ray Saunderson. GIVING the Real Recognition Way. (Recognition Management Institute, 2011).*

Tagognition: Everybody Wants It

Speaking from my own experience, I haven't met anyone (as Maslow suggests) who doesn't desire, on some level, to be recognized on the job. In all my years of HR, whenever an employee came to me with a problem or a request for advice, it almost always boiled down to some aspect of recognition that was missing—whether the individual was young or old, a cement truck driver or a geophysicist, or from Australia, Indonesia or Brazil.

Tagognition is Trans-Generational. It's true that employees joining today's workforce don't fear authority and have less respect for the boss than their predecessors. They admire winners and leaders and see quirky, inventive titles that reflect their competencies such as "Chief Geek" more respectful and real than "VP of Information Technology." And many of our younger colleagues are global nomads—that is, individuals who've spent a significant portion of their developmental years in another culture and have developed some sense of belonging to both their host culture and home culture, while not having a sense of total ownership in either. With this global influence, they may see their careers as a set of opportunities and experiences rather than a set career trajectory or salary grade progression. This means that companies have to pay far more attention as to how to attract, motivate and retain the new employee more than they did for traditional expatriates. And throwing more money and attractive compensation packages at them isn't necessarily the answer. There's an old adage in HR: "We recruit and pay for the position, not the person." While this may have worked in decades past, I'm not sure it will work with the Xbox generation. Today's "instant like" mentality is not in opposition to the company's focus on delivering value. In fact, the two match up perfectly when Tagging for Talent. By giving everyone the opportunity to give and receive Tagognition, everybody wins. For lots of companies, the main focus is to ensure a smooth transfer of knowledge in an aging workforce. The employees I've met, especially the older ones preparing to leave the workforce, have told me that it's much more than that. "For the first time in 36 years, I've felt recognized for my contributions to this monstrosity of a company," Wallace, a long-time machinist, shared with me. "When that young kid out of college told me 'thank you,' it meant more to me than the service pins they've been giving me every five years!" So I ask, what if we could say "thank you" every day?

Suffice it to say that some very large HRIS vendors and social software providers have already jumped on the recognition bandwagon, perhaps in search of greater profits versus a true application meant to help the business. Social recognition inside companies should be more than just employees earning colorful badges (which seem to be the latest trend) attributed by their peers. When added up, this collection of badges means winning virtual dollars or points to trade in for a television, microwave or other "prize." Perhaps this type of program is a modern spin on the five-, 10- and 15-year service pins or 25-year Rolex of years past, but Tagognition goes way beyond this and employees are smarter than we sometimes give them credit for.

Tagging for Talent is not just a virtual pat on the back; it carries much more impact and meaning. Not only do employees get feedback on their skills and behaviors but, ultimately, they get what they really want: consistent recognition, a fair process, more control over their destinies and an encouraging daily work atmosphere. Tagognition fits that job description on all counts. Take a moment to reflect and think back to when you were very young and somebody (a teacher, a parent, a friend) told you something that you did well (a paper you wrote, a song you sang, homework you turned in). How did it make you feel? Now think back to over the last 30 days at work and do the same reflection. Was it a colleague, a boss, an employee of yours? What did they compliment you on? What did they say or do? Where did they give you the feedback? How did it make you feel and why?

TAGTIME

CHAPTER 6

/tag time/ *noun.* when and where to attribute tags in the Tagosphere while ensuring sustainability.

Organize a team meeting. Set objectives. Prepare Succession Planning presentation. Conduct performance appraisals. Do salary reviews. Schedule travel to headquarters for meeting with the boss. Conduct interviews. Deal with M&A issues. Write training plan. Have lunch with a supplier. Meet the new hire starting at 9:00 a.m. Attend retirement party at 5:00 p.m. This is your to-do list, and it's only Monday... *and* you still have all of your normal work to do.

Okay, you get it. You see how finding hidden talent can be easier, how you can improve communication and add value through recognition... and now you're gung ho to create the Tagosphere in your organization. But you might be scratching your head about how you're going to find the time. We know that the pressure to deliver isn't getting easier with advances in technology; conversely, we're being asked to do more, faster. We have projects to launch and monitor, urgent and unexpected people issues to deal with, organizational changes being announced more frequently than in the past, ups and downs of the business to anticipate and manage, new strategies being rolled out from the top, and creative expectations surfacing from the bottom.

As the speed of doing business accelerates exponentially from year to year, we find ourselves simply trying to keep up. It doesn't necessarily imply that all businesses are doing well; in fact, in recent years this has hardly been the case for many companies around the world. But whether you work for a successful, high growth organization or one that is in dire straits, both have their own fast and furious rhythm requiring us to prioritize our initiatives, investments and human resources. So why would you want to take on something new like tagging when there are "more pressing" things to attend to? I hope the previous chapters have made the "why" and "how" clear enough; now let's complete the circle by looking at "when." I call it "Tag Time." Yet getting people involved in tagging is where you may need to put your efforts. And it's far more than asking employees to fill in their profile with their expertise in the company's HR system; it's got to be a lot more fun if you really want people to use it or play. Therein lies the beauty of the Tagosphere.

First let me assure you that Tag Time opportunities arise naturally and spontaneously every day and it requires very little technical or mental bandwidth to make a success out of it, because observing skills and behaviors is something we do automatically every day. We spend time chatting with others at the proverbial water cooler or coffee machine. We have lunch with people from our department or others in the company cafeteria. We share a few moments on the elevator catching up or exchange ideas before the start of a meeting. If we open our minds to the possibilities within the Tagosphere and maintain the right Tagitude, we discover a way to note a multitude of attributes that we are constantly observing but haven't previously had the means to constructively capture.

In Turkey, the prominent industrial group Eczacıbaşı has found peer based tagging of behaviors and skills to be both motivating and telling within their internal leadership program *Future Fit*. With 49 companies, more than 13,300 employees and a combined net turnover of $2.3 billion, the company is also faced with a war for talent in a thriving business environment. Their current and future leadership program participants see this activity as a unique way to identify talent and the company has been awarded for this by their HR peers.

Tag Time Starts on Day One

Oftentimes, we miss big opportunities to ingrain the basic rules and processes of our company in our employees during the first months after they join. Even though these early days are a well-known chance to capture fresh ideas and feedback from a new hire, not many companies take advantage of this window. Yes, some organizations conduct sophisticated orientation, induction, integration, product training or what I call "value programming" initiatives. However, once the recruitment process is finished (you know, the one that takes a lot of our time, money and experience and where the candidate is telling us everything about himself or herself to get the job offer), we stop asking questions. The mindset quickly switches to, "How soon can they start and how long will it take for them to be productive?"

We often need to interview many people for the same job opening. When we're finally able to make that call to announce "You've got the job!" everyone's happy. In fact, if you're a manager, you know that one of the best parts of your role is giving somebody that good news. But even more importantly, it signifies the starting point of determining success or failure with that new recruit. How we treat the person from the first day and throughout the first several months has a huge impact on that person's loyalty and integration to the company.

Experts call it "organizational socialization," the process by which an individual acquires the values, expected behaviors and social knowledge essential for assuming an organizational role and for participating as a member [Louis, 1980; Van Maanen and Schein, 1979]. Newcomers are particularly impressionable during their first few weeks in an organization, and thus are vulnerable to organizational influence regarding appropriate behaviors, values, attitudes and emotions [e.g., Schein, 1971; Van Maanen and Schein, 1979]. In other words, new employees will do *almost anything* the boss or HR department asks during those early weeks and months. They want to fit into their new environment, prove their worth, follow the company rules and regulations, and even make new friends. It's a given that we ask new hires to fill in paperwork for their bank accounts and benefits. Why not ask them to help us help them manage their careers with the company by having them tag their skills and talents? After all, it's a fresh start for everyone. Given the chance to show who they are and what they can do, employees will most certainly be interested in telling the company of their previous training courses, volunteer work, skills and competencies. We cover much of this in the interview screening process already; but other than entering basic data into an HR system of some sort, this all seems to be forgotten over time. If you think about it, other than what is documented on an employee's resume and post-hire interviews, the company loses track of what talent and experiences the employee has brought with them into the company. Even if the hiring manager has the memory of an elephant, who knows if this manager will still be managing this employee in the future or if the employee himself will have changed jobs, departments or businesses with the company. Isn't this how institutional memory walks out the door?

These first few months are prime Tag Time. It's the perfect chance to ask new hires to tag themselves and capture not only the competencies we've hired them for, but the attributes that make them the multi-faceted, complex human beings that they are. It also demonstrates that their new employer cares about their past experiences and abilities (not just how to squeeze as much juice out of them for the job). Drawing on authenticity research, we can see that organizational socialization is optimized when companies start by recognizing and highlighting newcomers' best selves at the very beginning of the employment relationship, when identity negotiation is a critical concern for both parties. "An individual's best self emerges from using and being recognized for his or her signature strengths, which increases his or her feelings of authenticity." [Seligman et al, 2005] Imagine the impact on the employee, as well as your company's reputation, when the new hire goes home and tells his friends and family: "I expected that they'd want to know my background when I interviewed for the job, but during my first week, they asked me to tag what I thought I was good at. It didn't seem to matter when or where I learned those skills. It's pretty cool, who'd have thought that my emergency preparedness merit badge from the Eagle Scouts would still be appreciated all these years later?"

So, this Eagle Scout immediately feels the positive effects himself. By being asked to highlight his strengths early on, he not only feels more authentic but also enculturated into the company. And the bonus is that he considers it normal behavior to observe and recognize talents of others in his new company going forward. If this awareness is ingrained from day one, imagine the new types of leaders we could develop. Roberta's story after being hired as a Financial Analyst for a large consulting firm tells a different tale. Before joining, she held the role of Fundraising Controller for a mid-sized, UK-based charity. Since starting with the consulting firm five years ago, the person who hired her has left and the HR VP has changed twice. This should be enough to get the point across of why tagging on day one is beneficial, but let's look further. Up until now, Roberta has enjoyed her new company and learning the consulting business. The organization has expanded by adding a nonprofit practice that helps charities establish their processes and funding models. The firm also has acquired a few charitable institutions as clients and is now struggling to find the resources to staff this part of their practice. If Roberta had been able to tag herself as "nonprofit," "fundraising" and "charity reporting and accounting" (among other skills and competencies), her experience and expertise would be visible to the firm. Roberta might be able to move and head up this practice or, at a minimum, provide valuable (and free) advice to her colleagues on what to consider or avoid. Alas, the consulting firm hired a consulting firm to recruit their "missing" talents. By the way, it's no surprise that Roberta is now looking for another job!

We, as talent managers, try our hardest and use all of our good will to know everybody in the company, but tagging from day one can make this easier and more realistic. Having new hires tag themselves in the beginning takes no extra effort on our part but gets important data into our systems immediately. As I said, it also sends a really important message to those new recruits: The Company cares. You can also predict the good that it will do for your employer branding.

After the Dust Settles

Soon enough, the newness of the lobby wears off, your desk becomes a bit cluttered and your inbox is overdue for a sorting. Yep, you're officially Employee #2498 and you have the badge around your neck to prove it. On any given day, you may observe Employee #2376 daring to ask that risky question in a meeting you *so* wish you had the courage to ask. On another day, you'll remember that training course where discovered that Employee #1276 was quite good at explaining the learning concept to others during the simulation exercise you both took part in. *Hmmm... I should tag her for that,* you'll think, and with a couple of clicks, you'll make good on that intention. Obviously, you don't think of your colleagues as numbers or as one-dimensional. Tag Time gives you countless opportunities to reveal their individuality every day. Tag Time can happen anytime and anywhere, which is increasingly important in today's virtual work environment. With all of the business travel I've done over the course of my career, a lot of what I've learned about colleagues and managers has taken place while on the road. The number of tags I could have attributed to my colleague, Kjetil, on that weekly flight between London and Oslo—and he could have attributed to me – would have made our talent profiles in the company much more interesting than the annual development plan and probably much more useful to the company. Whether in the waiting area at the airport, sitting next to the boss on the plane (don't you hate that?) or in the taxi ride to the hotel, I've discovered the most fascinating things about people. I won't go into what I've learned at the hotel bar... but even there, co-workers have shared their hobbies, charity involvement and other activities outside of their day jobs. In many parts of the world, a train ride for business can last several hours.

We often work on presentations, spreadsheets or strategic documents, and it's as efficient (or more) as an in-office meeting most times. Where carpooling is a frequent mode of getting to and from the office, between the discussions about the children and grandchildren, the tennis game over the weekend (where colleagues can learn a lot about each other, too) and gossip about the latest office romance, we also learn things about our co-workers that if the company knew, could help promote their abilities in a more efficient manner. During those commutes by plane, train, bus and automobile, we can pull up the tagging system on our smartphone or tablet and tag away. What about those sales presentations or project working groups? They're also opportunities to tag talent. The number of times I've observed people who are excellent in "timekeeping," "task mastering," "price negotiating," "deal closing" or "contract writing" are multiple. The top sales leader is already recognized by the chiefs because he brings in that "big deal" every year, but when we try to capture in a formal process what makes that person great, we struggle to develop a competency framework to describe this. It may just be that a person knows how to listen at the right moment in a negotiation, has a way of remembering the customer's birthday or anniversary, or is simply clear in explaining the opportunities and benefits that your product or service has over the competition. Those few moments after a presentation or group working session can be transformed into Tag Time. You probably can think of many more daily examples. These scenarios all work great when you're in proximity to your colleagues but what happens when the water cooler is three time zones away?

Who Moved My Water Cooler?

As the workplace evolves and managing virtual teams across multiple cultures becomes a way of life, we also need to be sensitive to the fact that Tag Time may happen at a distance. The workplace is changing dramatically as Robert, a single dad and leading U.S. marketing executive, knows very well. Working from home has been both beneficial to his company and his home life. Robert might need to pick his son up from marching band practice at 4:00 p.m., stop by the store for some last-minute groceries at 4:30 p.m. and be back to his home office by 5:00 p.m. for a call with his California clients. An increasing amount of communications and interactions via telephone, online meeting forums and a variety of enterprise video conferencing systems has meant that some of us, such as Robert, have had to adapt quite quickly to this mode of working; while for others, it's a barrier. The fact remains, however—with reduced travel budgets, the need to move ever more quickly in the marketplace across time zones, an increased emphasis on work-life balance, and a generation of developing leaders who are sensitive to the environment and carbon footprints—that this mode of working will only increase. As more and more of us find ourselves becoming members or managers of virtual teams, it also brings on a whole new set of challenges in terms of assessing dynamics, managing communication and fostering member participation. Since we've become more virtual in our interactions, without the benefit of in-person visuals cues we have also become more aware of the nuances of our interactions. Knowledge sharing is made even more crucial. When your colleague is a continent away and the time difference means their weekend has already begun, you can't walk down the hall, poke your head into his office and say, "Oh, I forgot to tell you about the test results of the new product formulation."

Working in virtual teams and across cultures and time zones has forced us to be more exact, clear and concise in the way we operate and communicate. It requires us to pay closer attention to how the other person behaves, delivers results or otherwise responds. The trade-off is that we now need to be more succinct and focused. This is perfect Tag Time. The Tagosphere is undaunted by the challenges of the virtual world.

Think about the last time you took part in a video conference call. You may have noticed that one of your colleagues leaned forward when you were speaking, and was expressive with his face and arm gestures when everyone was discussing your ideas. "All of these signals mean something and they are even more pronounced in this kind of environment," says body language expert Patti Wood and author of SNAP: *Making the Most of First Impressions, Body Language and Charisma* (New World Library, 2012). "You may observe people signaling their interest by smiling, tilting their head, furrowing the brow in concentration, and by leaning forward and blinking with excitement. They are 'up' for what you are saying, so their overall posture will be up and attentive as well." In this case, we are able to attribute tags like "bargaining" and "persuasion" to the strategy guy who convinces us to change our direction or the engineer who shares his screen and "teaches" us about a new product feature with "patience" and "knowledge."

When we use these tools that help us to connect remotely, we give off more body language and verbal cues to others so that we can create more clarity and ensure that we are understood.

So, whether the water cooler is just down the hall or 5,000 miles away, there remains plenty of Tag Time for everyone.

The Battle Between Training and Talent: a Solution?

Now, I'd like to focus on a particular area near and dear to my heart that can greatly benefit from Tag Time. Even with all of our good intentions to link training, development and talent, one valuable synergy is still lacking. I struggle to find an adequate model of a company that uses the classroom, a tiny yet effective laboratory, to identify talent. There seems to be an ongoing and thankfully evolving internal debate within the HR profession on where the actual role of talent identification should sit. Sometimes there's the "Resourcing" or "Recruitment" department taking charge for some or all of the candidate identification process. Then comes along the team from "Talent Development," which may also include portions of Resourcing but often it's just a specific population like "the Top 100" or "N to N-2," where the top dog equals N. And then there's "Learning and Development" or the "Corporate University." They have the role of taking the list of gaps and needs identified during the succession cycle or development planning process and creating training around these gaps. The annual talent review, for instance, highlights a need to improve a shortfall that the company sees in understanding change. In response, the talent team throws it over the wall to the learning team and says, "Hey, build us a change management course—yesterday!" So the learning team goes off and sources it, buys it, or builds it; then they deploy it, measure it and beg for money to pay for it. Meanwhile, in the classroom, what's being missed would be quite valuable to the talent team if there were a way to capture and share it.

When a company has a robust learning culture or company academy approach, it is oftentimes in the classroom where we start to see the attributes in people that might not be required in their current position or observed by the "official" talent departments. Time and time again, I've seen people displaying extraordinary competencies and behaviors in a learning setting that one would never see the participant exhibiting on the job.

Or as Charles Jennings of 70:20:10 fame (and former Chief Learning Officer at Reuters) told me: "We send our managers off to a leafy château in the country to learn something like leadership skills or change management. We should just send them off to the leafy château and ask them to work and solve problems for the company." Jennings, a leading thinker and practitioner in performance improvement, change management, and learning, isn't joking when he tells me this. "They would get a lot more done, we'd observe their talent and they'd learn from each other. Of course, that wouldn't go down well with many Learning or Talent people, though!" Charles and I admit that some organizations are beginning to put the talent and learning functions together, but there's another ongoing discussion about the interchangeability of talent and learning professionals. Can one do the job of the other more easily? Until now, we have missed a valuable opportunity to link the two. Except for when delivering services to fill development gaps, the Learning function is often too far removed from talent assessment activities. With tagging, it doesn't really matter. It's the employees themselves who can begin to identify the best talent in the company, whether they're in the Top 100 or not.

One example I can point to is a program on persuasion and influence that my company ran in Brazil. During the course of the three days, there was a role-play simulation that required people to volunteer for different parts, such as the Chief Financial Officer, Vice President of Sales, HR Director and, of course, CEO. One young, new graduate we'd hired quickly shouted out with enthusiasm: "I want to be the CEO!" I don't remember how well he played the role but I do remember that he was ambitious, assertive and courageous. If I would have had the ability to tag him at that time, I could have easily taken a few minutes to tag the positive qualities I'd observed in this young man. If we can imagine allowing people to capture these observations during learning events, I am absolutely sure that this long, drawn-out discussion about the ROI of training would eventually be so obvious that we'd be concentrating more on its content and applicability to business (and not its viability). Opportunities to observe the skills and competencies of our internal talent are all around us, we just haven't had a way to adequately and equitably gather the data—until now.

A lead facilitator from the respected international training company Wilson Learning told me, when I asked him about the potential for tagging in the classroom, that "having a simple way to capture the hidden talent that we discover in the classroom would be a huge benefit to my clients. During interactive and small group exercises, there is always a lot of discussion and side conversations. I might ask a question related to the content and participants often draw personal comparisons that might not normally come up in the workplace. Just the other day I had a participant from the legal department of a large company in my class. She was explaining to another participant that where she used to work, she was given a project to launch a communications plan for a new product. Nobody would have guessed this from her job title but since the training exercise required participants to reach for some of their unused skills, this competency was raised to the surface." This consultant concluded by saying: "with my line of work, I have the ambition to continue motivating leaders to enhance their interpersonal skills, break out of bad habits, and take their teams to higher levels of performance and job satisfaction. Giving people a way to identify hidden talents would go a long way in making this reality."

When employees attend training and are asked to complete course evaluations, besides saying the room was too hot or the food was too cold, they often report back on the "happy sheets" that they weren't sure why their boss sent them in the first place. I won't try to convince you that tagging will solve this problem but I'd like to think that if Tag Time is given by the instructor, perhaps at the end of each day or on the final "what did you take away" session of the course, participants will definitely see what was in it for them besides another break from the office. Why not take advantage of the opportunity?

Other Tag Time Ideas

New hire integration and learning events are two very basic and easy ways to bring tagging into the workplace. In speaking with companies around the globe about this idea, they expounded on some other creative and even fun ways to incorporate the concept. Here are a few of my favorites:

"Tag Me" Days or "Tag Your Boss" Days – This would be a day, week or special time when employees are asked to tag each other as a kind of contest. I especially like the idea of "Tag Your Boss" because it _gives permission_ to those employees who might otherwise be nervous doing this, and gives bosses a chance to hear something good.

Customer Tag Day – I like this idea of choosing an event or time during the year when customers are asked, with the help of their company contact (remember it's an internal system) to tag the strengths of their interlocutor in the company. This one's innovative because it creates a different, positive kind of relationship between the customer and company.

Tags of the Week – One Communications Director shared with me that he could see a weekly tag cloud being published in the company electronic newsletter as a means of bragging about a specific division or department that gets little recognition and create pride among the group. And why not post it in the lunchroom or other commonly used communication outlets in the company?

Signed with a Tag – This is a simple one but often forgotten. Add a link to your internal email signature to remind people to tag you. You might also include this link in your internal phone directory or company profile page.

Hi! Would You Tag Me? – Here's an idea where employees are given a simple card they can give out that says "Hi! Would you tag me?" For some people, this would be an easier way to request a tag than verbally asking. Also, the card could be customized with the person's name, a QR code or other personalization.

Tag This Meeting – An easy way to capture the talent we observe during a meeting is to give out a card, similar to the ones above (or even printed on the back of your business card), where we can write a few tags for each person. If you have back-to-back meetings, this can serve as a reminder to tag them once you're at your desk or have time with your mobile device. Similarly, if you work in a company that is project- based, you may have what is often called a "Lessons Learned" meeting to discuss what worked or didn't work. Unfortunately, the negative aspects of a project don't seem to be difficult to communicate but adding tagging to this meeting is a way for project team members to give positive feedback on strengths they noticed about fellow project members. Tagging can work in any kind of meeting, and wouldn't you find yourself paying attention differently than you do today?

Tag Swag – Want to create an event out of your team's talents and strengths? A T-shirt with an employee's personal tag cloud (and why not one of the entire company?) is sure to be a conversation starter. This can also be printed on coffee mugs, computer mouse pads or other items that your company uses. One trainer gave as a gift to participants in a five-month program a coffee mug personalized with each person's tag cloud accumulated from their classmates. The only phrase common on the cup was "You've Got Talent!"

Speed-Tagging — Another idea is to integrate a tagging scenario based on a format used in speed-networking (or some of you may be more familiar with speed-dating). This activity might occur during a weeklong team-building event for a small group of employees. More original than the usual bowling tournament or team cooking classes, managers might be inclined to go back to the company and promote tagging as an idea themselves.

Tagathon — Some companies have gone through a sort of game to give people a specific and short amount of time to tag as many people as possible. Their theory is that of a therapist's approach. Give people little time to over-think their responses and they will say honestly what they see as the talents of others.

What Tag Time Do YOU Have?

These are just a few implementation ideas; they won't all work in your organization, but hopefully they demonstrate the fun you can have in the Tagosphere. To help ensure success with the adoption of the Tagosphere, companies can get creative with any number of ways in which they educate their employees about making informed positive judgments and getting the most out of the tags they receive. The key is to make it dynamic, fun and desirable. Do you have an interesting Tag Time idea to kick-start tagging or ensure its sustainability in your company?

CONCLUSION

TAGOVISION

*"My three-year-old daughter just said this:
'A magazine is an iPad that doesn't work'."*

—Tweet from a mom

"The only group that can categorize everything is everybody."

—Clay Shirky

Julian, age 12, is quietly playing video games in front of the TV while I visit his mom at their home in Malta. What he is doing appears passive and an idle waste of time, but as I am to learn, there's more going on here than meets the eye. I express my fascination to his mother that Julian can follow the online gaming strategy in Japanese while skillfully toggling through mazes, mountains, and monsters without getting annihilated.

'How do you know what they're saying?" I ask, interrupting his gaming mania.

'What?" he asks, sort of annoyed. "Well, I know what they're saying because playing the game is teaching me Japanese."

Now I am really amazed—not just at how fast Julian's thumbs are moving but that he's mastering another language at the same time!

Julian says he wants to be an architect, something that he may or may not change his mind about, but he is certainly primed for a future that will challenge him to use all of his talents and not let the world slow him down. Soon he'll enter high school, then a university to be taught, molded and encouraged to develop his weaknesses while allowing him to discover what he really enjoys doing. Don't get me wrong—he'll learn a world of new concepts and skills, and if he's lucky, he'll have excellent teachers or professors that show him how to best use these self-actualizations to focus on his strengths.

Then one day, Julian will most likely enter some form of "workforce" to continue down the path so many of us have been down. He'll be indoctrinated into the firm's or company's way of thinking, forced to follow the rules of the hierarchy (unless he becomes his own boss). He'll be hired for his obvious skills and talents while his hidden ones will remain uncovered unless he's given a chance to express them.

But there is hope.

By the time children of Julian's generation enter the workforce, we will find that it is much more technologically and socially connected than ever before. Their bosses will have learned a whole new kind of leadership—one that engages employees more and takes into consideration the whole individual and their talents. We know that leadership is constantly changing, and maybe faster now than before. In companies we've begun to talk more about concepts like mindfulness and whether to employ a "Chief Happiness Officer," but this is a relatively new territory. It is also linked to the emergence of a new leadership paradigm: the "why first" (cf. Simon Sinek), the "employee first" (cf. Vineet Nayar), more leadership and less management (command and control), fostering collective intelligence, and so forth.

This brings us to how we need to lead differently and what Olivier Zara describes as Paradoxical Leadership in his book The Tea Strategy: Agility, Innovation and Engagement in a Digital, Uncertain and Complex World. Tagging talents are part of this new paradigm wherein knowing the talents you possess means that you can control which jobs you are considered for and the leader can be more agile and move talents around more quickly and effectively.

Zara explains that "a paradoxical leader is a leader who is able to understand and manage the paradoxes that multiply in the modern world." He presents the challenges that any organization must take on in the hopes of continual development in a digital world that is more and more uncertain and complex. For talent identification, the paradox is simple: HR must keep control (profess to be the ones who know the talents of all employees) while at the same time let go (allow crowdsourcing to help employees know each other directly). "Letting go" is a characteristic of this new paradigm where the main added value of HR is in the crowdsourcing, not in the administrative processes!

I call this new vision "Tagovision." On a grander scale, all of this tagging business isn't really just about using a system to write down talents, but about how it has the potential to evolve us to a point where we stop concentrating on the things we aren't so good at, or can't change, and instead empower people to use their inventory of talents in a way that brings happiness and success—no matter how one defines them.

It is also about creating a habit of recognizing the talents we exhibit or see in others. By doing so, we become better people and organizations automatically become more agile. Employee engagement then becomes more natural.

In this book, I've focused on Tagging for Talent in the workplace because it represents the obvious place and application for what I'm proposing. But some other non-traditional organizations have already seen the Tagovision. I've been asked to implement the tagging approach in areas that might not be so obvious. A large church would like to use this method to find ways they could help each other as a community. Somebody with strong talents in coaching could help them with marriage counseling, whereas someone who has carpentry skills could help them make repairs or guide them on finding the right contractor. Schools have approached me to assist them in helping their students develop more self-confidence in a world that gets harder and more complicated to navigate. A Boy Scout group has found tagging to be helpful in teaching respect and integrity to their young members. And there are many other groups that this approach can help, simply because it comes down to the human need for feedback to improve or develop further.

I hope that whatever you take away from my modest set of thoughts and ideas gives you the enthusiasm to focus on what you're good at, but even more importantly, what brings you happiness in knowing that you ARE good at many things. Tagability, Tagitude, Tagutation, Tagognition, and Tag Time are simple ways to do this and are also memorable, but what we do with the outcome is the only thing that really matters.

Put your talents to good use and be aware that what others see may just be the window to your future. At the same time, look for the good attributes in others.

Give recognition to yourself.

Give recognition to others.

This will expand your insights and do nothing short of creating a better world.

About the Author

Michael Salone is the CEO of 3-6TY ("three-sixty), a consulting firm which uses the power of the crowd to identify talent for organizations. He is an international HR expert with a Masters degree in Human Resource Management. Michael has worked for multi-billion dollar companies such as Alstom and Schlumberger and has helped clients such as Carnegie Mellon University, the United Nations, Total, Eczacıbaşı Group and Michelin identify the strength they have inside their organizations. His experience has brought him to all continents, observing the same difficulties companies have in quickly and accurately identifying talent while encouraging feedback and recognition. Michael is American, has lived throughout the US, London and Paris. He currently lives on the Mediterranean island of Malta where he enjoys renovating old properties in his spare time.